COLIN HAYCRAFT

COLIN HAYCRAFT

1929 – 1994
Maverick Publisher

Beryl Bainbridge   Andrew Barrow
Neville Braybrooke   Richard Brain
Melvyn Fairclough   A.C. Grayling
Richard Gregory   John Haycraft
Tom Haycraft   Mervyn Horder
Francis King   Hugh Lloyd-Jones
Brian McGuinness   Alasdair MacIntyre
Derwent May   Helen Muir
Elizabeth Rosenberg   A.L. Rowse
Oliver Sacks   George Weidenfeld
A.N. Wilson

edited by
Stoddard Martin

Duckworth

First published in 1995 by
Gerald Duckworth & Co. Ltd.
The Old Piano Factory
48 Hoxton Square, London N1 6PB
Tel: 0171 729 5986
Fax: 0171 729 0015

A catalogue record for this book is available
from the British Library

ISBN 0 7156 2681 7

Typeset with affection by Ray Davies
Printed in Great Britain by
Redwood Books Ltd, Trowbridge

Contents

✻

III. ENDINGS MERRY AND SAD

APPENDIX

Plates between pages 120 and 121

Preface

Colin Haycraft, whom Lord Horder ranks 'with the best of the strongly individualist publishers of the century', died suddenly on 24 September 1994. Nine days later, on the way back from his burial in Wales, I began to discuss with Beryl Bainbridge the possibility of collecting a group of memorial essays about him. John Haycraft, his brother, had already remarked that such a project should be undertaken, if at all, with speed. The stated reason for this was to preserve as much of the spirit of the man as possible before memory faded into half-legend. The unstated worry was that many of those who knew him best were getting on and, for some, what they wrote about Colin might be among their last words for print.

A list of literate friends was drawn up, with help from Nicky Badman at Duckworth. All were asked if they wanted to contribute; all but a handful did. The perceived need for speed forbade much direction about what to write. Some felt most comfortable with overall impressions; two rested on fine obituaries submitted elsewhere. One confessed that he had many things to say but had forgotten the details; another drew back from writing about the dead with the candour with which he spoke about him. Others – Richard Brain and Oliver Sacks, notably – responded to a gentle urge to focus on the period of Colin's life when they knew him best or were the only witnesses.

The result is a mixture. Some pieces are synoptic, others specific, a few nearly as revealing about writer as subject. Editing was largely a matter of collation and arrangement, with a gentle chronology imposed so that those who knew him in youth speak first, friends of his professional heyday in the middle and admirers of a younger generation toward the end. Inevitably, there are repetitions – about his love of the classics, his penchant for memorable sayings, his prankster-like wit; but little was cut. The writers included are too adept at weaving webs of words to unravel this from that. Besides, the motifs repeated either deserve re-emphasis or are gone into with different points to be made.

It became obvious that the whole should be left in informal shape, as a kind of scrapbook or prelude to a proper 'life'. One hopes for something like that one day; for, if ever a life deserved to be kept living, this was. To all who knew him, Colin conveyed vitality and abundance. If he was sometimes maddening, he was always generous, accurate, lovable and (though he would deprecate the term) quixotically *heroic*. His death has left an unfillable place not just for those who were close to him, but for everyone interested in publishing of acumen and verve.

Stoddard Martin

I

A Small Boy and Others

Francis King
John Haycraft
Elizabeth Rosenberg
Richard Brain

Francis King

Apart from the Porridgey Mass

From childhood, I had come to think of Colin as of a younger brother. When I was six and he himself was only a few months old, his father, a major in the Indian army, had been murdered by a sepoy. The sepoy had intended to kill not my Uncle Billy but another officer, then absent on leave. Why had he wanted to kill the other officer? It was never revealed at the time – there was open talk of promotion denied to the sepoy, there were also whispers of some kind of sexual imbroglio – and I have never been able to discover the truth since.

Learning of the tragedy, my father and mother endured a punishing journey in the hot weather across India from Naini Tal to Murree, eventually to return with the distraught young widow, Olive, my father's sister, and her two little sons, John and Colin. The trio were to stay with us for a few months before embarking for Europe, where they were to make their home with my paternal, German grandmother – if, indeed, a woman so nomadic, constantly moving from one hotel or rented house to another, now in Italy, now in Switzerland, now in France, can be regarded as ever having possessed a home.

Dazed by the tragedy, Olive spent much of her time in Naini Tal lying out on the bed of one of the two rooms which my father and mother had put at her disposal, either completing crosswords in the weeks-old copies of *The Times* which reached my father by sea, or reading novels. Then, suddenly, she would jump off the bed, change into tennis clothes and make her way to the tennis club or some private tennis party. A tennis-player good

enough to have played at Wimbledon and to have taken a set off
Suzanne Lenglen in a tournament in Nice, she deployed her
strokes with a skill and ferocity which made her unbeatable in
Naini Tal. Of the two children she took scarcely any notice,
leaving them to the care of a slovenly and far from clean bearer
whom she had brought with her. Both boys began to look sickly
and emaciated. My mother, reluctant to interfere, would none
the less sometimes venture, 'Are the children all right?' Olive
would reply that of course they were all right, the bearer was
devoted to them.

Eventually my mother could no longer stand aside; and fortunately, when she took charge, Olive showed no jealousy or re-
sentment. Both boys were suffering from dysentery – no doubt
the result of the bearer constantly stuffing them with Indian
sweets from the bazaar. They were seldom bathed or even
washed. The Indian doctor told my mother that, by intervening,
she had saved their lives.

As a result of having cared so tirelessly for the two boys during
this period, my mother came (as she once confessed to me many
years later) to think of them as almost her own. To Colin she felt
particularly close; and in the years ahead, when he would come
to London to stay with us, first from school or his mother's home
in Torquay to take part in some squash or rackets tournament
at some such venue as Queen's Club, and then from Germany on
leave from the Army, she always seemed to treat him not as a
yet another visiting relative but as a second son. No doubt
largely because of some subterranean jealousy over Colin, real
mother and surrogate mother came to think less and less well of
each other over those years. Olive, intellectual, sharp-witted,
sharp-tongued, would refer to my mother, adapting a line from
a then well-known poem by Frances Cornford, as 'the fat white
woman whom nobody loves'. My mother, gentle, warm-hearted,
moody, somehow learned of this, and that in no way improved
her view of a woman whom she would often describe as 'thoroughly selfish'.

During his childhood and adolescence, Colin was not handsome like his brother John, but beautiful. With his small, deli-
cately muscled physique, pale golden skin, high cheekbones and
slanting eyes, he could have passed for a Burmese or Thai. I

adored him, as did many other people. He himself, no doubt as a result of those bruising early years during which, after the initial tragedy of his father's death, his mother then suffered a prolonged nervous breakdown, seemed immune to any deep affections. I write 'seemed', since I should guess that in reality the affections were there, hidden from sight under a carapace of boisterous cynicism. Indeed, the only time when he showed any obvious emotion was when he lost some match. To win was extremely important to him. Even as a small boy playing tennis, he would position himself at the net and then slam ball after ball with the determination of a killer.

During that period before his marriage we were very close. We corresponded regularly; I visited him two or three times at Wellington, when he was a schoolboy and I an undergraduate; he stayed with me in the flat which, as a British Council officer, I occupied in Athens, subsequently travelling with me about Greece in a jeep which we hired, he the driver and I the navigator and interpreter.

Inevitably, with his marriage and my constant absences abroad, we saw less and less of each other. Relationships between brothers often follow that course: intense intimacy, every secret shared, during the early years, then a gradual drifting apart, even though the affection remains. I wish now that I had made more efforts to see him; and that in consequence, during his last years, our meetings had not been confined merely to lunch together in a restaurant every two or three months or to a rare family reunion, when someone was christened, married or buried.

His behaviour during one such family reunion seems to me particularly revelatory about his character. After the church funeral of my brother-in-law John Rosenberg, Colin travelled with John's widow, my sister Elizabeth, their two daughters and myself out to Putney Vale Cemetery in a hired car. As soon as the vast, ancient Daimler glided off, Colin began to deliver himself of a series of extremely funny observations about death and bereavement. Reluctantly we all began to laugh; we could not help doing so. But all of us felt, guiltily, that such laughter was hardly compatible with an occasion so sad. For Colin that laughter was, I am sure, essential. In no other way could he face the realities of mortality and loss. Not merely emotion but the expression of emotion terrified him.

In this, as in many other ways, he resembled my father. My father, too, was often described as 'heartless', not because he did not possess a heart but because he was incapable of wearing that heart on his sleeve or indeed anywhere else. My father would indulge in the same kind of derisive jocularity on the most solemn of occasions. He, too, hated any kind of hyprocrisy, not merely calling a spade a spade but using that spade metaphorically to bash on the head anyone whom he thought guilty of self-deception, illogicality, flattery or the fudging of an issue. Yet both men adored their families, however dismissively they might refer to them and however off-handedly they might treat them.

Since most of my life has been spent in the writing of fiction, it sometimes saddened me that, after an initial interest when he was young, Colin never bothered to read any of my novels. He was, of course, notoriously contemptuous of the novel as an art form, once remarking to me of A.N. Wilson: 'He's such a good biographer. Why on earth does he want to write novels as well?' Colin was the prototype of one of the two central characters in my third novel *An Air that Kills*. Having read that book, he told me 'I'm nothing like that!' and then gave that high-pitched, gleeful cackle of laughter which one so often heard in his company. In fact, he was very like that.

Most people's last days are sad, and Colin's were no exception. As he battled for ownership of the firm and, through his combative frankness, managed to land himself with a libel action, he maintained his reckless air of insouciance to the public at large. But it was all too clear to me that he was really on the rack. That his months on the rack killed him, I have no doubt at all. The firm was more important to him than anything else in his life. The prospect of losing it filled him with anxiety, despair and rage.

Yet even during that last clouded period, he could still be 'tremendous fun' – as my mother would describe him. During what was to be our last lunch together, he brushed aside my queries about the firm, to launch into a series of increasingly entertaining anecdotes. As he concluded each, that high-pitched gleeful cackle would cause other diners to turn their heads to stare at us.

He was someone at whom people often stared; and he deserved to be stared at, since, so intelligent, iconoclastic, independent, courageous, learned and witty, he always stood out from the porridgey mass around him.

John Haycraft

A Head Full of Stories, A Heart Full of Songs

With Colin, I still measure: 'Oh, he died four weeks ago', or 'It only happened two months ago.' Soon it will be years, if one is alive, oneself; it will only be a memory of his voice, his quizzical look, his habit of roaring with laughter so infectiously at his own jokes that one laughed at the laugh. Sometimes I think of ringing him, and suggesting lunch as I did before September 24 1994, to hear that deep-voiced 'Hullo!'. I can't really believe it's not possible to make arrangements to meet any more.

We were never very close as adults, partly because he lived in north London, and I in the south; partly because I travelled abroad a lot and he preferred to stay at home; largely because our interests were very different; academically, mine was history; his classics. I remember him asking my mother at the age of five: 'Mummy, was Marie Antoinette a man?' On Gibbon's *Decline and Fall of the Roman Empire*, which was one of his passions, we coincided.

As children and adolescents, we were closer. I remember going to Cornwall on holiday with him and a good friend. They began to cavort perilously on cliffs. 'Come back!' I shouted. My stomach twisted with anxiety, but not for my friend, however much I liked him. I realised then that my bond with Colin was almost umbilical and protective.

We were brought up by a single parent. Our father was killed when Colin was three months, and I was two years old. He was a major in the Indian Army. There were various versions of why the Sikh sepoy shot him in the heart on a firing range. However, I think the truth was that the Sikh had asked to be promoted to *naik* (corporal) and had been openly refused by my father and the commanding officer. Afterwards, people said the sepoy was mad, but open humiliation and the failure to get promoted was presumably as galling to a sepoy, if not as 'important', as it would have been to one of Napoleon's generals.

At the time, Colin and I both had dysentery but did not die because, as our mother, Olive, maintained, she changed from Cow & Gate baby food to Allenbury's! Olive tried to forget her misery by absorbing herself in tennis, almost fanatically. Cut off, she decided to become a tennis champion and we lived where there was sun, or covered tennis courts: in Switzerland, Italy and the Côte d'Azur, where Olive sliced one game from Suzanne Lenglen and partnered Gustav V of Sweden in a tournament.

Although she had only her army pension of £400 a year, and £150 of her own, rates of exchange were then good enough for reasonable hotels and nannies, one of whom, Daphne Owen, we both liked and another, Molly Todd, we both disliked because she was hot tempered. I remember vaguely her throwing our treasured wooden railway engine out of a hotel window at Nice because one of us had done something wrong. At Nice, too, we were beguiled by a little White Russian girl called Tanya, who made us believe there was a giant cooking human bones in a neighbouring white house with smoke coming out of the chimneys.

In the hotel, which was called the Tsarevitch despite the Russian Revolution, there was also an English boy who was terrified of rubber, whom we pursued spasmodically with our black, inflated cat.

In Switzerland, we were both very young and I remember only getting into trouble for pushing Colin off a low wall into the snow. Inevitably, at that age, my seniority of two years made a difference. Also, there were two of us for one parent, and I tended to elbow my way in.

The years in Italy were bliss for both of us. We stayed in Alassio, on the Genoa coast, when I was six, and Colin four, in a Hotel Salisbury, with extensive grounds of relatively wild countryside. As we were not yet at school, we spent the days swimming, or trying to play tennis, building great palaces of palm leaves, waging war on the nettles with cactus swords, and warring on the *bambini* of the neighbouring village. Indeed, our Uncle John, my father's only brother, was so worried by a photograph which my mother sent him of us fighting with staves against the *bambini* on the roof of a crumbling house, that he asked if Olive was sure we were being brought up properly.

Retrospectively, Colin, himself, was not in doubt. As he said in his address to the Classical Association, in April 1994:

> It is to this period of my childhood that I owe my love of the classics.
>
> My earliest memories are of the Mediterranean vegetation (some of it of course post-classical) — mimosa, figs, artichokes, olives, vines, cypress trees, lemon groves, fields of narcissus — and the noonday heat when
>
> > The lizard with his shadow on the stone,
> > Rests like a shadow, and the cicada sleeps
> > *(Oenone)*

In Alassio, the hotel was run by the Signori Arighetti who had no children, and would murmur '*Belli bambini*', as they ran their fingers through our hair when they passed us on the stairs. They even allowed us to fish for goldfish in the tank outside with bread and a window hook until, finally exasperated by failure, we removed the stopper and were confronted by an empty tank of squirming fish who had to be hosed down by the gardener to survive.

One evening, Colin was sitting on his pot while the grown-ups were downstairs for dinner, when suddenly, the pot broke and gashed Colin's left buttock which began to bleed profusely. I substituted my own pot and went down to summon help which came in the form of our mother, Miss Owen, the Arighettis and various maids. The room was soon full of gasps and exclamations: '*Ay? il poverino!*' '*Cosa faciamo?*' '*Proprio terribile!*' Finally, someone went for the doctor who sewed up poor Colin's wound, the thick scar of which he had all his life. I used to tell him he should put it under 'Special Characteristics' in his passport.

At this time, Miss Owen had to leave for England. As there were only a few months before we moved to France, Olive hired a peasant woman, called Maria, who, to our disgust, alluded to jam as '*ca ca*' and used to pee sonorously in her pot in the room she shared with us. In the evenings, we used to take refuge from her in the hotel kitchens to escape being put to bed. Here, we had an alliance based on previously finding a nest full of eggs which we gave to the kitchen maids. Now, in return, they would push us into an empty cupboard immediately we heard Maria on the stone stairs. 'Where are the *bambini*?' she would ask. The kitchen maids shrugged their shoulders. We would be listening silently from the cupboard, and would emerge after Maria had gone, to be to be given jam omelette which was a speciality in that part of Italy.

During this time, we were visited by various relatives from England, our Aunt Lucille who gave us each a shiny five franc piece, our Uncle Cyril who gave us a pot of hydrangeas, and, frequently, by Olive's mother who was originally from Bavaria and still spoke with an accent. She was small and bent, with prematurely white hair, and always wore black clothes and a choker, and used to entrance us with her stories, mostly based on German fairy tales. Olive played the piano, and we would sing Schubert songs with her. 'Granny has her head full of stories,' once said Colin, 'and Mummy has her heart full of songs.'

One day, we moved to Menton in France which was close to the Italian/French border. There, I went to school at the Lycée in the mornings, and Colin was looked after by our new nurse, a pretty girl called Nini Lang, who came from Strasbourg and couldn't speak a word of English, which was good for us.

During this time, I must have got on badly with Colin as for some reason I bit him. Nini was so incensed that she made me go into the hotel dining room at lunch-time with a card on my back, '*J'ai mordu mon frère!*' Although I don't remember Olive's or Colin's reactions, I do remember the self-conscious agony I felt at being exposed in this way to the hotel guests. This was slightly relieved by Nini also being subjected to a placard. When we went to the beach by the promenade, she would undress visibly behind the rocks, and then leave us in order to go off and flirt with her *camarades* who, one day, pinned a notice '*A louer*' to her back.

Neither of us had any idea what this implied but it did seem a strangely appropriate revenge. Later, in accord with the conventions of the time, Nini was sacked for sleeping with Albert, a curly haired waiter at the hotel.

At Menton, we also both had violin classes with a severe Italian lady called Sgra. Gherardhi who organised a concert given by her students. Colin at this time was small and cuddly without glasses, and at the concert he played confidently and beautifully, while I forgot my notes and stumbled through my piece. Perhaps it was envy that made me bite him!

In 1936, we left to go back to England as I had to attend a prep. school. The special scholarship we both had because of our father's death on active service only applied if you were over nine. So I went to a school close to Wellington College which only cost my mother £10 a year, while Colin went to one in Folkestone where she had to pay the full amount. In the summer, Colin went to visit the family of our grandmother's sister, in Ulm, in Germany. He shocked the family by saying Hitler was a fool, which they were afraid might get to the neighbours. Another example of Colin's forthrightness and natural boldness was his delight at umpiring at tennis matches. I still remember at La Baule where we spent a holiday, this long umpiring ladder with Colin perched diminutively on top, pronouncing the score in French which he had learnt fluently from Nini. Another example of his initiative occurred in Paris when, aged eight, he went out all by himself to buy a jacket in a department store. Strangely, I cannot remember Colin having toys such as small cars, or tin soldiers, or a stamp collection such as I had. Perhaps he read a lot.

My prep. school was foul, full of little boys who were aggressive because they were afraid of each other. When Colin arrived in 1938 at the age of nine, I fussed in my determination to protect him. I was anxious that he follow convention as far as possible so as not to get into trouble. But he ignored me and forged off on his own. Much of the boys' attitude was bluff, and he realised this and ignored them. He was a 'natural' with cricket and football which, as was inevitable at most English schools, earned him respect. Academically, he was also outstanding, and ultimately gained a scholarship to Wellington, which meant that Olive did not have to pay for his education at all.

When we were at Wellington, the war had broken out, and the school was no longer – like its reputation – a serious, hierarchical Army school. Many of the masters were university dons who were disqualified for health reasons from joining the Forces. There was a good art section under K.G. Green who had designed sets for Covent Garden; and an enthusiast, Maurice Allen, was in charge of music in which Colin participated, playing the flute, which he continued until he was fifty or so.

Here we went our different ways. I wrecked my knee in rugby, seriously injuring the ligaments, which meant running was my only *forte*. Colin excelled at the more individual games such as squash and rackets, ultimately winning the Public School Rackets Championship. I climbed a more 'administrative' path and became Head of the School and Head of Athletics, while Colin followed his natural exuberance to a greater extent, among other things being court-martialled for dropping his rifle into the lake during a Corps field day. Together, we also became involved in a number of 'pranks', including going home a day early for the Christmas holidays – for which only I was beaten when we returned, as the older boy and therefore responsible. When I was promoted to Prefect there was a problem in those corporal punishment days. Beating one's own brother for frequent misdemeanours smacked almost of incest, so Colin was beaten by the master in charge of our House instead, and complained this was worse as, in comparison, I was a much weaker beater!

Academically, we both reached the Sixth form but Colin had only one companion in the Classical Sixth, and together they shared the not inconsiderable classical inheritance of the school: some thirty prizes a year which they divided between them. I remember early on at Wellington, he became totally absorbed in the classics. In the holidays, he would study till 2 a.m. and get up late. Both of us ultimately got awards to Oxford, although while mine was an Exhibition, Colin's was an Open Scholarship to Queen's.

Meanwhile, we had changed our home from London to Torquay, which had covered courts, and which Olive felt happier about during the war. We abandoned life in hotels and Olive rented a small house in St Marychurch. That last summer of

1938, Olive also got into Wimbledon but, unfortunately, was knocked out by a seeded player in the first round.

With us lived our grandmother who had gone through the full gamut of belonging to a respected nationality when she married in 1887, to living through two world wars in which the Germans were hated to such an extent that she pretended to be Swiss when she went shopping. Both Colin and I kept this family secret without thinking about it. Philomene, as she was called, seemed older than her years, not yet seventy. However, she detested speaking on the telephone and thought the radio went both ways, telling us not to make rude remarks when Hitler was giving a speech, as he could hear us. Yet as far as I know, Colin was not really aware of her smell of mothballs, or the plumes of black smoke emerging from the kitchen whenever she tried to cook.

Even I, as his brother, did not entirely understand Colin's attitude to other people. Perhaps he was not really interested in them unless they could talk about the classics, often dismissing them too easily. I think this was partly because of his passion for Latin and Greek, which continued throughout his life. Whether this was partly an escape from his childhood where he didn't feel favoured by Olive, or felt over dominated by me, I shall never know.

Perhaps he should have become a don. But in his day there were few posts available and, despite his double first at Oxford, his brief spell as Cecil King's assistant on the *Daily Mirror* daunted any selection board.

Elizabeth Rosenberg

Irreverent Prankster

My earliest memory of my cousin Colin is of him as a young baby, brought with his elder brother John to my parents' house in the foothills of the Himalayas after the murder of their soldier father on the Northwest Frontier of India. Not surprisingly, their mother, my father's youngest sister, was distraught and in a state of shock after her husband's death and it was my capable mother who took charge of the two boys, both of whom were suffering from severe dysentery. My mother always maintained that she had saved their lives.

Some years later, when my parents were on home leave in the mid-thirties, they rented a house in Eastbourne and John and Colin were then staying in a hotel nearby. It was here that the three of us used to play the game of Mothers and Fathers, and Colin was regularly obliged to be born to me on the ping-pong table in this hotel.

At the outbreak of the war, my father also now being dead, my mother and her children were on holiday in Devon and the Haycrafts and my paternal grandmother were then living in Torquay, my aunt being an enthusiastic tennis-player who chose this resort because of its covered courts, on which she could play all the year round. We visited them there, and I remember Colin's concern – not shared by the others – that we should be properly fed, and also his own skill as a tennis-player – a diminutive figure racing about the court and seldom missing the ball.

When Colin went to school at Wellington College he began to spend part of his school holidays with us in our flat in

Kensington. Perhaps memories of my early role in Eastbourne as his mother influenced him now in his relationship with me, because although I was only a few years older then he was, he seemed to regard me as a mother-figure. I'm afraid that I gave him his first cigarette, after which he took up smoking and, indeed, got into trouble at school for this habit.

On an early visit to London he was taken by me and my brother Francis to see *Peter Pan*. When the question was asked 'Do you believe in fairies?' Colin, even at that age a sceptic, shouted 'No!' We told him that this would mean that Tinkerbell would die, so he stood up in his seat and shouted even louder 'Yes, I do! I do!'.

When he was an undergraduate at Oxford I used to visit him. I remember that we often played a game in which we leant out of the windows of his rooms on to the street below and invited passers-by to come up. One of these was a sailor who said he was a member of 'a pool'. Colin found this idea irresistibly funny: 'a pool of se(a)men'. He laughed at this joke in a way only he could do.

In the early 1950s, my husband John and I were living in a second-floor flat in Prince of Wales Drive, Battersea Park. Being rather short of money, we used to have a lodger and when Colin was working in London, he lodged with us. We all got on very well together and we used to have long discussions late into the night, usually in the kitchen. On one such occasion Colin and I were sitting there talking, when John, who had turned on the bath, came in. He joined in the conversation, oblivious, as we were, of the water running in the bathroom. There was a ring at the front-door bell, which Colin, the only one still dressed, went to answer. He returned looking puzzled. 'That was the man from the ground floor. He wanted to know if we had a flood. I said of course not.'

Colin played the flute in those days and John was a good pianist. We also had a friend who visited us who played the clarinet. These three played trios, which gave us all much pleasure.

After a time Colin left us to share a flat in Chelsea with Richard Brain. One of Colin's delightful ideas was to have a Roman banquet. Delicious food and drink was provided all day while the guests came and went, lolling on the floor and talking. Fortunately we were not expected to use a vomitorium.

One evening Colin came across the river to visit us and suggested we walk back to Chelsea to have coffee in the Kenya Coffee House in the King's Road. When we had sat down at a table he discovered he had left his cigarettes in the flat in Markham Square, just round the corner. He said he would fetch them and come back. He never returned. The next morning he telephoned me to apologise. 'You see, I met a wonderful girl.' He had been introduced by his landlady to Anna Lindholm. He was anxious for my approval.

Colin and Anna were married at Anna's parents' home in Wales. John and I travelled there with Richard. (We, his mother and an aunt were the only members of Colin's family to attend.) It was the time of petrol shortage and I remember how Richard used to switch off the engine on down hills and coast – also how he had to keep stopping as my aunt was car-sick.

Colin and Anna returned to live in Markham Square and it was here that their first son was born, whose godmother Colin had asked me to be. Both my husband and Colin, though on the face of it not believers, seemed to have an intimate feeling for the rituals of the Church and the sacraments. Neither of them objected to being married in the Catholic Church or having their children baptised in it. Colin's first son was to be baptised William Pius. When his baptism took place he was already quite large and heavy: I was so nervous of dropping this precious child on the stone floor of the church that I begged Colin to stand close to me and be ready to catch him if he fell. Luckily this did not prove to be necessary.

But Colin was nothing if not irreverent. When John died four years ago he travelled with me, my two daughters, my brother and my niece – now sadly also dead – in the funeral car from the church to the cemetery. All the way Colin made jokes and told stories, many of them scurrilous, and all accompanied by his inimitable laugh. My niece was profoundly shocked, but I did not mind: knowing him as I did I felt it was entirely in character and quite endearing. Besides which John, who had great affection for him, would have understood, and I felt sure that Colin's irreverent attitude was by no means out of keeping with the occasion.

Richard Brain

At Oxford and in Chelsea

Colin was my oldest friend. We each said of the other, after some years had passed, 'He is my oldest friend.' We first met, in early December 1946, as competitors for Classical Scholarships at Queen's College, Oxford. He had come up from Wellington College and I from Shrewsbury School for the few days of the examination; we were lodged (as was the whole troop of scholarship candidates) in rooms of undergraduates who had gone down for the vacation. Colin pays deserved tribute, in his Presidential Address to the Classical Association of 1994,[1] to his VI form master at Wellington, Alan Ker (pronounced 'car'), who had been an Oxford Mods don: 'To be taught as a schoolboy by a man of this calibre was an amazing piece of good fortune.' I had had very similar good fortune to be taught by a Classical VI Form Master at Shrewsbury, Stacy Colman, who had been an Ancient History don at Queen's in the early 1930s but who was a Mods man at heart.

Colin had the advantage in that he was, at that time, the sole member of the Classical Upper Sixth at Wellington (not a school with a special prestige in Classics) and so had had from Alan Ker virtually tutorial teaching, especially valuable in Greek and Latin prose and verse composition; whereas, at Shrewsbury, Stacy Colman had more than a dozen boys in his Upper Sixth. Both our VI Form Masters must have known that Thomas Erskine Wright – Tommy Wright – at Queen's had the reputa-

---

[1] See Appendix. (ed.)

tion of being the best Mods Tutor of that time in Oxford, and the hope of receiving his wonderfully scholarly and Scottish teaching may well have been what brought both Colin and me to try for a Queen's award in Classics. (In the event, when in 1949 we went up, T.E. Wright had left Queen's to become Professor of Humanity at St Andrews.)

Each day we sat our exam papers, along with other schoolboys trying for scholarships not only in Classics, but in Modern Languages, History, etc. In the evenings the candidates met each other at meals in Hall, and perhaps in the Buttery or in the Tabs Room (Taberdars' Room, as the Queen's Junior Common Room was named). I don't recall if other boys from Shrewsbury were candidates at Queen's then, but I was very soon struck by the liveliness and originality of two Wellingtonians: the gangling, shambling figure of Robin Chanter, with his darting eyes and tongue, who was doing the Modern Languages papers; and the short and perfectly formed, nimble figure of Colin Haycraft. I soon realised that Colin was my match as a classical scholar, and my principal rival.

Robin and Colin were friends, and we talked each evening till late. Colin and I discovered much that we had in common: very early childhood in India; the ending of our parents' marriages (his by the murder of his father when Colin was but two months old, mine only that very year by their separation, to be followed by divorce); a home in Torquay, where Colin and John's mother still lived, and where I had spent school holidays at the vicarage of my guardian, the Rev. Gilbert Backhouse, and his wife and son from 1939 to 1942 (I think Colin and I had Torquay acquaintances between us); and of course our schooling in the Classics. Alan Ker had given Colin an introduction to Harold Cox, the Philosophy don at Lincoln College, and Stacy Colman had given me one to Maurice Platnauer, the Old Salopian classical scholar who was Vice-Principal then at Brasenose. I went to tea with Maurice at B.N.C., and it comes back to me now (as I write) that after he had dined with H.H. Cox (and possibly some subsequent visit – to a friend or a pub) Colin returned to Queen's to find the gate closed and himself locked out, the porter gone. He somehow called Robin's and my attention, and we helped him to climb into the college through an upstairs window.

Colin was then, as ever, adventurous, impudent, and irreverent of rules. I think he tore his trousers; but that didn't matter much to one who, throughout his life, often omitted to button, or zip, them up.

At the end of that week, we went back to our respective schools, where term would soon end and boys return to their homes, some of us agog to hear the Scholarship results. Haycraft and Brain were jointly awarded the top Classical Scholarship at Queen's, Oxford. The first letter I received from him, in his exquisite, just-so-stories, widely word-spaced handwriting, from Great Tor, Teignmouth Road, Torre, Torquay, is dated 'a.d. XIV Kal. jan. MDCDXLVI [for non-classicists, that's 18 December, 1946]':

My dear Richard,
Let me congratulate you from the bottom of my heart. I rang Queen's College this evening and heard the gladsome news; but I still do not know how Robin has fared. I feel that nothing better could have happened: it all seems like the will of some wise and benevolent fate: it seems like another bond in a friendship which has been born in good auspices ...
[a paragraph about Robin Chanter]
I arrived back home today, after a pleasant journey from Berkshire, and am settling down to a leisurely Christmas to free my brain, burden my stomach, and indulge my lungs. I am now peacefully relishing my pipe, which I can assure you is only 3 parts affectation.
I hope you will excuse the shortness of this letter, but as you know in exultation the mind is never constant to one thought for long, but flits from idea to idea and from sense to sense. I feel so happy both for you and me; and happiness is [one of] the hardest things to express in writing.
Love,
Colin

By New Year's Day we were both in London and met again a few times during that first week of 1947. I was staying, as I quite regularly did when I came to London in my school holiday, at

Liddon House, attached to the Grosvenor Chapel, where Canon Cyril Pearson – who had married my parents in Calcutta nearly twenty years earlier and christened me there – was Priest-in-Charge and Warden. Colin was perhaps staying with his Aunt Faith, the mother of Francis King and his sisters. It must have been then that I went to Queen's Club to see Colin play rackets – or was it real tennis? I certainly met Francis there, and Michael Meyer, who was also a real-tennis player. Colin had been Public Schools Rackets Champion (in both singles and pairs) the year before.

Colin had left Wellington at the end of the previous term, but I went back to Shrewsbury for two more terms. We had both opted to do our National Service (lasting two years) before, rather than after, being up at Oxford, where we knew we would both meet again in October 1949. Colin must have received his call-up papers and joined the army early in 1947, while I was still at school. I joined up that September. I believe Colin did take the War Office Selection Board examination for potential officers – his brother, John, was, probably at that time, a 2nd Lt. – but failed it (perhaps deliberately: Colin later told a story of dropping his bren gun or rifle in mud or water during the WOSB). Instead, he joined the Royal Army Educational Corps and within a year was Sergeant Haycraft.

We met once, while we were both in the army, I an officer cadet in the Royal Corps of Signals, on 27 February 1948. I was on leave, and I dare say Colin was, too. I came to London for the day from Henley-on-Thames, and we met and had coffee together and later went by tube to Richmond for a walk by the river. We visited Kew Gardens; and I still recall with shame the haughty attitude I took with him at that time, never present in our relations before or since. But was I not then an O/Cdt. and Colin (though a Sgt. and paid more than I was) a mere NCO? Such was the force of military hierarchy.

Later that year we were both stationed in BAOR (the British Army of the Rhine) in Germany, but I feel sure we didn't meet again until we had each finished our National Service (Colin months before I did) and went up to Oxford for the Michaelmas Term 1949. I remember much looking forward to seeing Colin again. I went to Queen's on 6 October, and I guess probably he

did too. At the end of one of our first evenings back, after we had
met other Freshmen and renewed acquaintances made at the
Scholarship examination, I recall lingering in Colin's rooms on
the ground floor of Back Quad Staircase III while he told me
tales of the experiences with women he had had while in Germany. Looking back on it now, I associate that period with the
end of our – or at least his – adolescence; at any rate, it marked
a new *etape* in our continuing friendship.

During our four years at Oxford, reading Mods and Greats, Colin
and I shared all our tutorials, listening to each other reading our
essays to our tutors: J.D.P. (Jim) Bolton for Mods, Guy Chilver
(who was our Moral Tutor from the start, and with whom – and
his ebullient wife, Sylvia – we soon became friends) for Ancient
History, and A.D. (Tony) Woozley, the best and most humane of
them all, for Philosophy. They were Fellows of Queen's, but we
were seconded to dons in other colleges for particular subjects for
the odd term: during Mods, only to F.C. Geary at Corpus Christi
for verse composition; but in Greats to J.D. Mabbott at St John's
for politics, to Harold Cox for some Aristotle, and to Tony An-
drewes in New College for some ancient Greek history. Colin and
I also attended certain lectures together (John Griffith on
Juvenal, and Eduard Fraenkel, the Corpus Professor, on the
Agamemnon; and later, H.T. Wade-Gery, the Wykeham Profesor
of Ancient History, on the Athenian tribute-lists); but after a
while Colin hardly went to any, having learnt to study much
more intelligently in libraries or in his own room.
    After taking Mods in early March 1951, Colin moved in with
me to share a set of rooms in the Front Quad on the Queen's Lane
side, for that languorous first summer term of our reading
Greats, my companion for the preceding two terms having preferred to move into lodgings. Colin's and my private and social
lives were, however, largely separate – not least in sporting
activities. Colin eventually won Blues at rackets, squash and
tennis; actually we did sometimes play tennis together, in dou-
bles at Lady Margaret Hall, with Eleanor Forshaw, the sister of
a Salopian school-friend of mine, and her best friend, Carole
Robertson, who played for the Oxford women's tennis team. A
fairly balanced game could be attained with Colin and Eleanor

vs. Carole and me. Otherwise, I could only beat Colin at shove-ha'penny in the Tabs Room, where I suspect my winning owed more to Colin's free-spirited drinking and talking than to any tangential skills of my own.

That summer term we also went to ballroom dancing classes together (upstairs on the Broad, opposite Balliol, somewhere), to little effect upon either of us. This was chiefly in preparation for the Commem Ball, when term had ended. I forget who Colin's partner was. I remember one girlfriend in Oxford of whom he saw quite a lot, especially that he described her in Latin as 'ore longo, lunis exiguis' (she had a generous mouth, but her finger-nails had practically no moons visible).

That summer vac Colin had a holiday, arranged in conjunction with his cousin Francis, in Greece. About the same time, I went to France, first on a walking-tour with John Nottingham, an inexhaustibly vigorous (but short-sighted) Salopian hero of mine, in the Auvergne, and afterwards canoeing down the Allier and Loire with Maurice Platnauer. In due course I got a letter from Colin dated simply 'Monday' from 'British School of Archaeology, Odos Souedias, Athens':

> ... It really is wonderful in Greece though I've been here only a few days. The 'plane arrived at midnight on Friday – six hours late. I looked out of the window as we passed over France but I couldn't see you as you were so small. Our route was Nice, Brindisi, Athens ...
>
> I shall stay in Athens till Wednesday to meet Francis' plane from England, and then I hope to make a tramping tour of central Greece – Thebes, Boeotia, Delphi – cross the Corinthian Gulf to Patras and then to Olympia, Bassae, Tripolis, Misthra (*sic*), Mycenae, Nauplion, Corinth & back to Athens via Eleusis. The last week I shall go north to Salonika. It sounds all very glorious but whether I shall have enough cash or not is a different matter ...
>
> I am glad you are enjoying your French trip. Probably the reason why John Nottingham is so energetic is that he can't see the top of a mountain till he gets there. You ought to show him a map before you start. I'm looking forward to

hearing about your trip next term, especially with Maurice which ought to be great fun. Don't push him in ...

It was fun sharing a room last term and I'm very glad you thought it was a success too. It was good ending the term on such a pleasant note with the Ball. I hope we manage to tute together next term.

Prof. Trypannis' [Trypanis'] mother speaks with a definite Chian accent.

Love,
Colin

On 16 September, he wrote to me from his home in Torquay:

Thanks very much for Cook-Wilson ... I hope for your sake you haven't found philosophy as incomprehensible as I have: for me it's rather like remembering a musical theme − I get so far and then a blank, and I start again from the beginning and so interminably. I'm still waiting for that sudden flash of light which I remember at the age of 11 after I'd been doing geometry for two years. But they say in philosophy it usually doesn't come till the week before 'Greats' ...

Going to Greece has just about invisibilated all my financial assets − I simply haven't got a penny left and still owe £9 for my Battels. I've sent in a plea for extenuating circumstances, viz inability to pay. Poverty is so degrading (didn't Juvenal say something about that?) and I just go on borrowing money from my mother with little hope of paying it back. The main trouble is that I must smoke ...

Colin had got a First in Mods, worked very hard in our final year (1952-3) − so that I saw him very seldom − and, despite his earlier anxieties about philosophy, and thanks to Tony Woozley's excellent teaching of both of us ('Richard is full of error, Colin; can't you persuade him?'), he was again awarded a First in Greats. In the summer after we went down, he sent me a slim volume of T.S. Eliot, writing on 24 August (from 51 Teignmouth Road, Torquay):

My dear Richard,

I'm taking an awful risk sending you this book (a) because you might not like Eliot, (b) because (more likely) you may have it already on the shelves. I don't remember seeing it there though. I wanted to send you something and this was the only suitable thing I could find in the local Smith's (I always think poetry is the best sort of book to buy cos one can read it more than once – unlike novels) ...

I'll write from the States when I have a fixed address. I sail in 10 days.

Very best luck,

Love,

Colin

From at least my last year at Oxford, I had been encouraged by Charles Monteith to try to make a career in publishing. A Fellow of All Souls and a lawyer, he had given up the Bar and joined Faber & Faber, where he eventually became one of that firm's most distinguished editors and rose to be its chairman. In the drift and insouciance of youth, however, I made no determined effort to approach publishers; and I earned by first year's living as a Classics master at a public school. Halfway through it, I was fortunate in being given an introduction to Roger Machell, Hamish Hamilton's partner, just when they had decided to take on an editorial assistant, and was offered a job to begin that September, 1954.

Charles Monteith now again greatly helped me by introducing me to Christina Muir at her house in Wilfred Street, where he was already a lodger. She had a small room at the back of the house which she let to me from the time I began to work at Hamish Hamilton Ltd. Her house became my home for eighteen months. Christina worked at Longman's, still very much a general as well as an academic and educational publisher and with offices in central London, where she was secretary to the editor John Guest. Among her colleagues at Longman's, whom I got to know as well, were Colin's cousin Elizabeth Rosenberg (her brother, Francis King, was one of John Guest's novelists) and

Elizabeth Russell, who worked for Michael Longman on the firm's religious list.

In early 1955, Colin was doing his journalistic apprenticeship with Mirror Newspapers Ltd., of which Cecil King, another cousin of his, was chairman. That February my pocket diary shows that I saw Colin fairly frequently, at 22 Wilfred Street in the evening – the musical *The Boy Friend* and the film *Seven Samurai* are noted by me on dated with his name, so we probably went to them together (I saw *The Boy Friend* three times that year) – and on 27 February a family gathering of Colin's mother, his Aunt May, and John and Elizabeth Rosenberg, as well as myself, met for coffee at 10.30 a.m. and saw him off from Victoria Air Terminal for his flight to Nigeria, where he was to work on the Lagos *Daily Times*, owned by the Mirror Group.

Colin can't have spent more than eight months in Nigeria. Certainly by 9 November I was having dinner with him and the Rosenbergs; perhaps he was then staying with them in their flat on Prince of Wales Drive, Battersea. He was by now starting his auspicious-sounding job as Personal Assistant to Cecil King, at the *Daily Mirror* headquarters in Geraldine House, Fetter Lane. (But the reality of that job gnawed at Colin's emotional and intellectual entrails.) Meanwhile we must have met regularly, since sometime that winter we decided to share a flat together.

Liz Russell (of Longman's) lived with her Aunt Maye, Miss Lambert, at 33 Markham Square – one of the most handsome Chelsea squares adjoining the King's Road. The second and attic floors of the house had been converted as a flat with its own kitchen, bathroom and lavatory, but it was not separated from the main part of the house – the two principal floors and the basement – where Aunt Maye, Liz and her brother, Johnny Russell, lived. Aunt Maye was glad to let the upstairs flat to friends of friends of her niece's. We used the front door and the staircase and inevitably came to know our landlady well. She was known as Aunt Maye to all the denizens of Markham Square and had lived in No. 33 for over a quarter of a century. Despite diminishing eyesight and the need for a stick as a support even in walking about the house (she was in her seventies), little escaped her curiosity or her kindness. A devout worshipper at St

Mary's Bourne Street – not the nearest church, but the 'highest' – she was a much-loved, slightly formidable saint. Colin and I were treated virtually as family friends, tenants though we were.

We moved in on 25 February, 1956. On the second floor of the house was a quite large living-room, which we shared; I had the bedroom at the back of it; the third floor contained a narrow kitchen, Colin's bedroom at the front and the bathroom behind. From these top-floor windows, on the front side, we could get out and sit in warm weather on cushions or on the parapet, high above the square and its well-kept garden.

That summer Colin met Anna. She was working at the delicatessen on Elystan Place (we used to call it Chelsea Green), behind Markham Square; in those days there was a path beside the bomb-ruined Congregational church at the end of the square, and that shop was thus the nearest provisioning place for more or less instantly edible food (neither Colin nor I was much of a cook). They have often told the story of her selling Colin a fruit pie when he intended a meat pie for himself, only to discover his mistake when he heated it to eat and flavoured it with tomato or Worcester sauce. Anna first started coming to the house shortly after; and Liz Russell remembers how one day that hot summer she and her brother and Anna and Colin and I climbed out of our attic window and sat on the roof (and probably drank beer) and I read some Keats aloud to them. What can it have been? Perhaps, by contrast with the heat, some of 'The Eve of St Agnes'; or, since we were given rather to puns, 'O Attic shape! ...'

I don't know if that day was earlier or later, but the first mention of Anna in my little diary is on 23 July; and thereafter occasions 'with Colin & Anna' occur frequently. The Russells had a party the following day, a week later the Fletchers (John Fletcher was another Wellingtonian contemporary of Colin's, who had also been at Queen's with us). We three went to these together, and subsequently to others. What I chiefly recall is Anna's beauty and discernment, and the happiness of the pair of them; Colin was constantly amusing company, and Anna seemed to double the pace of his jokes and the length of his own laughter at them. More and more often she came to our flat. By October her stern and striking self-portrait – she was already an excellent and immediately recognisable painter – hung over the sitting-room mantelpiece. I feel sure the standard of cooking much improved. None of us had much money, but a good deal of beer was brought in and drunk – and we went out much to parties and pubs.

The wedding followed late that autumn. It was arranged to take place at Penmaenmawr, Anna's home town in North Wales; and I was asked to be best man. One of my charges was to look after Mrs Haycraft senior; I remember we had to stop on the road between Shrewsbury and Oswestry as we drove to Wales from London, as she was car-sick. (From her home in Torquay, though she continued to play tennis there, I doubt whether Colin's and John's mother ever went far by car.) It was a practical ceremony, on a chilly day of wet-slate sky; and the reception was in a teashop-restaurant of the little town that in summer was still a seaside resort. We men, including Anna's father, Mr Lindholm, wore morning clothes; and I presume I made a speech – which I know I should have meant every word of, even if it wasn't as witty as Colin and Anna deserved.

In mid-January, Colin and Anna gave a party in our flat, a post-wedding reception for London relations and friends who'd not gone to Penmaenmawr. Among them were Queen's College, Oxford friends, including Guy and Sylvia Chilver, Harvey McGregor, Gerald Kaufman – who was then also on the staff of the *Daily Mirror*. Cecil King himself came; he had given a wedding present, of two perhaps valuable, but not much admired, Chinese vases. There also came Gene Baro, a beaming, generous and rotund American, who was a friend and protégé of the novelist Marjorie Kinnan Rawlings, and a would-be critic and writer himself; I had met him at the home of my boss, Roger Machell of Hamish Hamilton's, and through me Gene came to know and be very attached to Colin and Anna. (In the 1960s, he was their tenant in a top-floor flat at 22 Gloucester Crescent, on his lengthy annual visits to London from the USA.)

Gene became a frequent guest of ours at Markham Square, himself bearing always gifts of food and wine – and host to us out. He was almost a joint host when we decided to celebrate the

2,000th anniversary of the murder of Julius Caesar with a party we called Caesar's Banquet. Supposedly Roman food only was eaten, sheets were worn for togas, and we all reclined on cushions; the entertainment began at 3 p.m. and lasted till 1 a.m., and it was on 16 March (a Saturday). The Ides of March was, as it happened, Aunt Maye's birthday, and I'm sure she came up to inspect the feasting in the upper part of her house.

Colin must have left his *Daily Mirror* job by then, I feel, and was at home most days, very well employed in reading the whole of *The Decline and Fall of the Roman Empire*. About then, also, I introduced him and Anna to Zélide Teague (I had met her through getting to know her brother Mickey in his last year at Oxford); she was an artist, book-illustrator and jacket-designer, and her boyfriend at that time was Tim Simon. A fortnight after Caesar's Banquet, I went with Colin and Tim to Tunbridge Wells for a day with Zélide and her parents in their house in Hungershall Park.

Colin was applying for academic posts, for which he was well qualified; but his *Daily Mirror* employment may well have tainted his attempts. My diary notes for 17 April, 'Colin's Interview', and for 22 May and 31 July, 'Colin to Oxford'. On other occasions, I've recorded going to exhibitions with Colin: Stubbs in March, Musée d'Art Moderne in April. We saw Zélide and Tim Simon fairly frequently that spring and summer; Tim was at the Curwen Press, run by his Uncle Oliver, in Plaistow, promoting and selling their high-quality printing. In early June, Colin and Anna and I went to supper with Charles Monteith. The world of publishing was much around us; and Colin must continually have seen how much I enjoyed my job at Hamish Hamilton's as the assistant to the two editing Directors of the firm.

William Haycraft was born on a bright summer's morning, in Colin and Anna's bedroom on the top floor of 33 Markham Square. As William is regularly reminded when he meets me, my one involvement at the start of his life was to receive from the midwife a brown package containing the after-birth and take it down to the basement where I asked Aunt Maye if I might burn it in the coke boiler – permission granted with her usual cheerfulness (certainly a first in her house). He was christened William Pius after the Pope at the time; and I was a (strictly secular) godfather. Shortly afterwards the nascent family left Markham Square and moved to Hampstead, needing a home to themselves. Jeremy Noble, who had also been a lodger of Christina Muir's in Wilfred Street, moved in to share the flat in Aunt Maye's house with me – though only for three months, since I myself went to live elsewhere later in the autumn.

Colin and Anna took a flat in Belsize Crescent. They had very little money; their meals depended substantially on the onion and the potato – though William never lacked for mother's milk. Colin worked for a while on the *Observer* as an assistant to the gossipy, but kindly and knowledgeable William Clark on 'The Week', then the back page. A year or so afterwards, however, he became, like me, an editor in a publishing firm, The Bodley Head.

I think I was only once able to help Colin specifically in his career thereafter, and that was in the early summer of 1959, when I suggested to him that he ask J.R. Ackerley if he might consider his novel, *We Think the World of You*, for publication by The Bodley Head. The manuscript had been turned down by Secker & Warburg and Chatto & Windus (previous publishers of Ackerley's work) when it was offered to Hamish Hamilton. There I was the first to read it and was captivated; I wrote a report on it for Jamie Hamilton in which I described it as 'in better English prose' than any novel he had published in the five years I'd been an editor – perhaps not tactful on my part; anyway he found the book too sentimental about both the dog and the working-class young man, and declined it. I told Colin at once of my enthusiasm turned to disappointment, and he got in touch with Joe Ackerley and was able to have the novel published the following year. It received excellent reviews, and in 1962 it won the W.H. Smith Literary Award.

Colin went on to work at Weidenfeld & Nicolson through most of the 1960s. Then, in 1968, he and Tim Simon (who had by then married, by coincidence, Hamish Hamilton's niece Sue) took over Gerald Duckworth & Company. Colin's career there is related by others in this book. But I am glad and thankful that, in divers and diverse ways, I helped to bring publishing into his life.

*

I heard of Colin's death the day after it happened last year (the day of Zélide's eldest daughter's wedding). I had to go to Spain three days later, on a holiday arranged and booked long before, with a friend in his nineties; so I was absent both from the Requiem Mass at St Etheldreda's and from the burial service in the churchyard at Pennant Melangell. But I was glad to learn that among the hundreds who crowded the church in London were Liz Russell and Robin Baird-Smith, who had been colleagues at Darton, Longman and Todd; they came together to attend that service. I feel that is a good augury for the future of Colin's firm, Duckworth, of which Robin is now managing director. And on 10 December, eleven weeks later, I paid a lonely visit to place chrysanthemums (the appropriate Italian offering) on the grave of my oldest friend, where he has been put to rest in a valley that is close to being a part of heaven.

II

Individualist Publisher

Neville Braybrooke
Brian McGuinness
George Weidenfeld
Mervyn Horder
Beryl Bainbridge
Oliver Sacks
Hugh Lloyd-Jones
Alasdair MacIntyre
A.L. Rowse
Helen Muir
Derwent May

Neville Braybrooke

Mallard Extraordinaire

Colin Haycraft had something of Father Christmas about him. He loved giving presents. I remember him turning up at our house in Hampstead with bottles of whisky, cigarettes and chocolates. 'How is the book going?' he would enquire. The book in question was *The Letters of J.R. Ackerley*, which I was editing for Duckworth. Even as a boy of thirteen, he loved bringing presents – and I can remember him arriving at my mother's flat in Kensington with sweets and biscuits. In wartime England, with rationing at its severest, these were indeed treats.

When he was a schoolboy at Wellington, Colin used to spend most half-terms with his Aunt Faith, who was the mother of Francis and Elizabeth King: they lived within easy walking distance of us, and I can recall our flat door-bell ringing and Colin saying to my mother: 'Can Neville come for a walk?' I was some five years older and in the Home Guard, waiting to be called up. At Ampleforth, during my last terms there in 1941, I had launched with some friends a little review entitled *The Wind and the Rain*, which was to run until 1951.

After our walks in Kensington Gardens, Colin would come back to tea and ask if he could see any of the manuscripts which had been sent in to the magazine. About ten arrived each week. He was interested in books and authors, and could be extremely scathing. Once when I handed him a batch of poems by a poet whose surname was Cook, he skimmed through them and returned the verdict: 'The chap should have been named "Washer up". The poems are nothing but the dregs of other men's sinks.'

In those days Colin entertained hopes of becoming a novelist like his elder cousin Francis King, who had published two novels while up at Balliol. But this ambition of Colin's had faded by the time he himself went up to Oxford. None the less at Queen's College he showed himself to be not only a brilliant and erudite undergraduate, but an all-rounder at games: he became captain of the university's squash rackets team and gained a double first in Mods and Greats.

I married in 1953 – three years before Colin. Sometimes he would come with my wife to Richmond Park, where she would organise races between her eleven-year-old daughter Victoria (by a former marriage), and Colin and myself. Out of gallantry we had to let Victoria and her friends win. Afterwards we would retire to a local caff for tea and baked beans on toast. On these occasions Colin would sometimes break into Latin – and we would look mystified. 'Don't you know Cicero?' he would chide us and, before we had time to speak, he would answer: 'Of course you're Catholics who've been brought upon on ghastly Church Latin.' He loved to tease; he also loved to air his knowledge. In the caff one afternoon he announced to us and everyone present: 'Saint Jerome had a dream in which he found himself being whipped for placing Cicero before Christ.' Colin was full of odd pieces of information, especially about the classical world. He could easily have gone on to hold a chair in Greek or Latin at any university.[1] In fact, it took him nearly a decade to decide where his vocation lay.

During this period, he worked as a personal assistant to Cecil King, the Chairman of the *Daily Mirror*, where among other things, Colin encouraged him to back the *London Magazine* – though he thought John Lehmann a poor choice for editor, his own candidate being Kingsley Amis. Next Colin joined the *Observer* as one of the staff writers – but was not happy in the job. Nor did a commission from Penguin Books to translate Erasmus come to anything.[2] Finally Colin was to discover that his true talents lay in publishing. But his first entry into publishing was as the publicity manager to The Bodley Head, and a very strange

---

[1] There is a running controversy about this: see also pp. 43, 90 and 99. (ed.)
[2] Anna Haycraft is still looking for the part of the Erasmus manuscript which Colin wrote: it appears to have been lost. (ed.)

publicity manager he proved to be. Much of the time he spent telling his directors what dreadful books they were bringing out and suggesting how much better it would be if they reprinted the novels of William Gerhardie, or commissioned a life of Ovid or Pope or Cavafy. Colin's job, however, was to take authors and literary editors out to lunch and so promote Bodley Head books. One author, who was a prostitute and brought out a bestseller under the title of *Streetwalker*, he took to Kettner's in Soho. Later he told us: 'Several of the diners looked as if they could kill me. They were probably her ex-clients.'

In 1971 Colin became the Chairman and Managing Director of Duckworth. To a firm founded in 1898, with a backlist which included Belloc, Ford Madox Ford and D.H. Lawrence, he gave a fresh and highly individualistic look. In the 1976 catalogue, for instance, there are quotations in both Greek and Latin. Under the heading 'Some Mallards Imaginaires' there are items which include a photograph of W.G. Grace walking back from the wicket after making a duck, and a Second World War recipe for Mock Duck, which was made from sausage meat, dried sage, and one onion: a spoonful of marmalade could be added as '*a pretend orange sauce*'. At the end of the catalogue there is the proud boast that Duckworth is a firm whose editors employ accountants, rather than *vice versa*. This was a thousand miles away from the world of conglomerates, which was then beginning to emerge. Colin's wife too – the future novelist Alice Thomas Ellis – played a significant role in building up the fiction list.

The Times in its obituary remarked that Colin was 'conscious of being a good deal cleverer than his fellows' – and he definitely used this to his advantage. His method for promoting Duckworth books was simple but effective. Here, in summary form, is how he explained it to us:

1. Take a literary editor out to lunch, ply him (her) with drinks and use such words as 'unique' and 'outstanding' to describe the books being published.

2. Elaborate in particular on the merits of one. For example, praise the historian Richard Cobb for his sense of place and

his understanding of the relationship of man to his rural and urban landscape.

3. At the end of the meal, over coffee and brandies, re-cap on what you have said, but making it appear that your guest thought of these things himself (herself). Use phrases like: 'As you were saying, Terry, Cobb really is unique ...'

4. Suggest a reviewer, with the comment: 'I know he (she) admires you and your paper ...'.

In the case of my edition of the Ackerley letters, I remember he rang my wife on the eve of publication to say: 'All the reviews are lined up' – and then rattled off the names of the reviewers: Spender, Holroyd, Angus Wilson, Grigson, Paul Bailey, Isabel Quigley. Colin maintained that literary editors were grateful for having reviewers suggested to them. Indeed, he took a very cynical view of the literary world, seeing it as a mixture of a racket and a lottery. Yet despite such cynicism he cared passionately about Duckworth books and standards there were of the highest order. I think of de Sainte Croix's superb analysis of *The Class Struggle in the Ancient Greek World*, F.V. Parsons' history of *The Origins of the Morocco Question: 1880-1900*, or Michael Dummett's masterly study of Frege, the founder of modern formal logic. How well I remember Colin declaring at a dinner-party in his house that Frege was a philosopher on the same level as Kant and Leibniz. And when Colin spoke, people listened: he had authority and wit and a powerful intellect. On a BBC radio in 1973 he told an interviewer that he would never publish anything which he despised – and he kept his word.

As an editor Colin was meticulous. When he invited Joe Ackerley to prepare for him a personal, corrected copy of his novel *We Think the World of You* (1959), he asked him not only to restore the cuts insisted upon by the libel lawyers at The Bodley Head, but to toothcomb the text for any other errors. At one point Ackerley consulted him as to whether it might not have been better at one passage if he had used the word 'repressed' as opposed to 'suppressed'. 'Second thoughts', Acklerley had added, 'but you did say "toothcomb".' Colin told him to stick to 'suppressed' because 'it was more English'. Apparently Ackerley had been reading a number of American psychological books in which the term 'repression' had featured repeatedly. Certainly preparing Ackerley's letters for press with Colin had its hilarious moments. My typist was an elderly woman, who had been highly successful in transcribing Ackerley's handwriting: but, in a 1966 letter, she was defeated and typed a sentence about E.M. Forster preferring to talk about 'hat-stands' rather than robins. The real word was 'cock-stands'.

Although Duckworth published many specialist books, Colin would stress that they were essentially 'general publishers'. In the 1980s when he accepted a guide to belly-dancing, he was well up to promoting it. For its launch, he had a small stage set up in the firm's office and wore an electric bow-tie that flashed on and off. When the time came to present the star of the evening, he stepped forward and said: 'Ladies and Gentlemen, here for your umbilical delight is Miss Tina Hobin.'

On another occasion, on the two hundredth anniversary marking the day when Edward Gibbon completed *The Decline and Fall of the Roman Empire*, Colin, dressed as Gibbon, read from the balcony of his house in Gloucester Crescent the passage where the great historian describes his feelings on taking everlasting leave of a book which has been such an old and agreeable companion. For Colin, Gibbon remained England's supreme author: the historian's cynicism, no less about pagan than Christian practices, in Colin's opinion lifted it from a work of history to one of literature. In A.N. Wilson's view Colin had a look of Gibbon, but was more handsome than his hero. On the day before the celebration I sent Colin a postcard on which I copied out Robert Lowell's comment to Elizabeth Hardwick: 'What? You haven't read Gibbon? How is that possible, you with such a fine pair of legs?' Colin pinned the card up in the hall.

There is no doubt that Colin enjoyed baiting and teasing women. When he learned that my wife approved of the writings of Teilhard de Chardin, he informed her: 'You have the soul of a housemaid.' During the 1970s when he brought out a paperback edition of Charlotte Wolff's study of lesbianism entitled *Love Between Women*, he was delighted when I passed on the praise of two lesbian friends who had read it: ever after, he referred to their home in Hampstead as 'Radclyffe Hall'. Colin loved trailing his coat and would sometimes go up to feminist groups, as I once saw him do at a party given by Majorie Watts, the daughter of the founder of PEN, and ask if any of them knew a gay woman friend who would like to write an autobiography under the title of 'The Divided Skirt'. Yet despite such mockings of womankind, he was a devoted father and, long before it was customary to do so, attended the births of his children. He and Anna were united in their opposition to women priests.

In a pub in Earls Court in the 1950s, Colin and I once found ourselves in conversation with a group of queers, as they were then called. Suddenly he looked at his watch: 'Half past six. I should have been home an hour ago to wash my baby.' As we left, they stared at us with incredulity. But Colin was speaking the literal truth, for the baby was Joshua, his second son, who in his late teens was to die as a result of a fall through a corrugated glass roof.

Josh was my godson and when I used to visit him at the Royal Free Hospital in Hampstead, I would find him lying in a coma, unable to speak and wired up to the heavens, as indeed perhaps he was. I would read him entries from my diary and, when I mentioned seeing someone whom we both knew, he would squeeze my hand which I had placed in his. In the room where I am now writing this, I have a photograph of him; next to it I have put a picture of an angel by Ghirlandaio. Anna dedicated one of her novels to Josh and Colin commemorated his death in a moving poem in Greek.

The last time I saw Colin was at my wife's funeral in June 1994. The night before he had brought up to our house bottles of whisky and cigarettes. Three months later he himself was to die of a stroke in University College Hospital, in North London.

His funeral was held at St Etheldreda's, Ely Place, on 30 September, the feast day of St Jerome. Nineteen years before on this day he had published a life of the saint by J.N.D. Kelly, which he would refer to as one of the stars in Duckworth's star-studded crown. Across the review-slip he had added: 'September 30th is Saint Jerome's feast.'

When I entered the church, it was already packed and I managed to slip into a back pew where Francis King and F.V. Parsons were sitting: we had all worked for Colin at different times. In the homily the celebrant spoke of his old friend, drawing an affectionate portrait of Colin wrapped in a rug, sitting before a log-fire and studying Latin texts. In the hospital Anna had sent for a priest and insisted that her husband should have the last rites. The Mass was in Latin and after the final blessing, the choir sang *'In Paradisum deducant te angeli ...* May the angels lead you into Paradise ...' My mind went back to our young days in Kensington Gardens and Richmond Park. How short are the days of youth! I thought as well of the many Duckworth books which Colin had given me – enough to fill several shelves. I remembered too how once we had argued for over an hour about the translation of a line from Sophocles. Colin was a perfectionist – and finally he accepted this version for the title-page of *The Letters of J.R. Ackerley*: 'We have only a little time to please the living, but all eternity to love the dead.'

Brian McGuinness

Queen's Man

Colin Haycraft, Open Scholar and later Honorary Fellow of Queen's College, died suddenly just when he was preparing to attend the Old Members' Dinner of 1994. He was the son of an officer in the Indian Army, shot by a sepoy during Colin's infancy, apparently by mistake. His paternal grandfather was a professor of some originality. The mother who was left to bring up the two boys (John Haycraft, founder of International House, was the elder brother) was perhaps more interested in lawn tennis, which she played to what would nowadays be called a professional standard. She came from an Anglo-Irish family with every claim to distinction except wealth. It is possible to trace many elements of this varied heritage in Colin's character and life.

Brought up at first largely abroad (in mature years he left England only for the Frankfurt Book Fair), Colin, as the son of an officer killed in the line of duty, went to Wellington College; and Wilfrid House sent him to Queen's. He had already made an impression at Oxford as the clever and irreverent schoolboy cousin of Francis King (already a novelist). Thomas Erskine Wright, more serious, wanted him to decide whether he preferred Latin or Greek Prose Composition. Actually he preferred Verse Composition to either, a preference of a piece with his love of technique as such – a Rackets champion, he looked down on the easier games of Lawn Tennis and Squash (though he was to get his Half Blue in all three: Real Tennis was the pastime of his later years); somewhat privately he would play the flute.

Two years as an Education Corps sergeant intervened, not perhaps what one would expect from a Wellingtonian, but this was a Wellingtonian who dropped his rifle in the pond – because it was heavy – and who generally did the unexpected. He came up in 1949. The moustachioed veterans had gone down, Jim Bolton was now Mods tutor, and the last pre-Robins decade was beginning. Platnauer and Balsdon had their Socratic circles, Syme and Ryle lectured with every assurance of being at the centre of the world, and the voice of C.M. Bowra was heard in the quad.

Colin loved the college and he loved its classical traditions. He ended his presidential address to the Classical Association with Edgar Lobel's noble lines from the Second War Memorial. But he was not an easy undergraduate for his tutors. Personally a friend, yes, but so quick as sometimes to seem arrogant. Between Guy Chilver and Harold Cox there was an exasperated bet that he would get a Third in Greats. In fact he got a First, as he had done in Mods. He had a powerful mind which would cut through nonsense and received ideas. But the obituarists who say he could easily have been a don are perhaps unaware of the patience, the *Sitzfleisch*, and the tolerance of boredom that is necessary for that humdrum profession.[1] When non-academic aspects are also considered, Colin was an Admirable Crichton, with his many Blues, his clubbability, and his inventive humour, not always merely verbal: the motor-horn sounding from his Queen's Lane corner room and holding up the traffic in either direction marked him as an early ecologist, and in fact he never drove – except in Nigeria, where it was most dangerous. It is difficult to find Queen's contemporaries who were not friends or at least admirers and he appreciated their qualities – as his later publication of Oliver Sacks and Sydney Afriat (among others) shows.

His first job was as personal assistant to a more distant cousin, Cecil Harmsworth King, the creator of the modern *Daily Mirror* (this is what took him to Nigeria). He chafed under this, and could hardly bring himself to get up to go to the office; and

---

[1] See also pp. 36, 90 and 99. (ed.)

perhaps his employer chafed too. Another spell with the *Observer* proved more useful for his later life.

Once in the literary world Colin entered publishing and learnt the trade in the usual way. One task was to abridge Gibbon's *Decline and Fall of the Roman Empire*, perhaps the book that this book-lover most admired: 'We had to omit the decline,' said Colin. But slowly the individuality of approach which irked some superiors marked him out as a natural, and George Weidenfeld wisely gave him a free hand with the World University Library. Colin's career as a commissioning editor was launched and he became a familiar common room figure, telling dons what they ought to, what they could, and what they really wanted to write.

For, successful though the Weidenfeld series of introductory books was – one thinks of Richard Gregory's *Eye and Brain* – Colin's real triumphs came when he took over the established house of Gerald Duckworth and showed the university presses how to meet the expansion of those days in both supply and demand for academic books. At first he had a partner in Tim Simon and a mentor in the former proprietor Mervyn Horder (with whom his relations were like those with his Queen's tutors); but Simon died (a blow in many ways to the new ownership) and before long Colin was taking all decisions – it was amusing to hear colleagues innocently saying, 'I'll send it to Duckworth and see what they think.' 'They' was Colin and what they thought was that a book of originality should be published, even if it was long and whatever price it must be sold at.

And how original the books were! One remembers the historian who began his book, ' "I will tell me," I said, "all about Robespierre" ', and the pre-historian who traced the dependence of man on the sheep through the ages, and many other books that perhaps no one else would have published but which shaped our thinking. Without Duckworth books the last twenty years of Greats subjects would have been sadly lamed. Here much was owed to *il lungo studio e'l grande amore*, much also to the advice of Hugh Lloyd-Jones and other friends; for Colin knew just whom to listen to, and for how long. The readers' reports of conventional publishers did not fit his style. If the book was any good at all, the author would know better than the 'reader' what it was that he wanted to say.

Yet Colin's own contribution to the books was considerable. He enjoyed (when it was not hopeless) the task of copy-editing. His maieutic skill in encouraging an author can best be illustrated from a classic of modern philosophy, Michael Dummett's *Frege: Philosophy of Language* – Colin would allow no account of this in the preface. The book (as Dummett explains) had been laid aside, even for decades, but Colin sent Emma Fisher up to rootle it out of shoe-boxes and kept Dummett to a schedule of chapter-writing. Dummett had always published a sufficiency of important articles, but this was the beginning of his career as an author of books.

Even had Colin's list consisted only of his Queen's College authors, it would have been a distinguished one: John Kelly's *Jerome*, Fergus Millar's *Emperor and the Roman World*, Jim Bolton's *Glory, Jest and Riddle* (not simply an act of *pietas*, for this was an inspired publication, with a profound effect on those to whom it spoke), George Temple's *100 years of Mathematics*; books too by Tony Honoré, John Matthews, Siegbert Prawer, by the contemporaries mentioned above, and so on. Robert Blake made a selection of some of Disraeli's less shocking utterances; and Deborah Blake, a daughter of the college, saw many of these books through the press.

The history, all too *événementielle*, of the firm of Duckworth would itself be worthy of a book. Colin insisted on remaining a general publisher and original literature continued to feature on his list, Beryl Bainbridge being perhaps his best known author. His parties were occasions when two half-worlds, the academic and literary met; the mediocracy could not be excluded but was kept in its place. A hospitable house in Camden Town, a cottage in Wales, and a moving toyshop of a book-factory were, it seemed, always open to authors, who became additions to an already large family. In recent years the factory was the centre of a series of cliff-hanging episodes involving the financial future of the firm. Colin could not easily find, or when found brook, a new partner. He seemed to have arrived eventually at a solution which left him in effective control, but it is hard not to believe that the struggle shortened his life.

The fairly recent honours came in time – the Presidency of the Classical Association – he had certainly deserved well of the classics – and an Honorary Fellowship of Queen's College. Fellowship, as a quality, was perhaps the greatest of his many gifts. There was no one with whom one would more willingly tire the sun with talking; and it was good straight talking with intellectual power behind it, reminiscent of his idea of how to play tennis with a certain sort of opponent, 'Hit the ball very hard straight at them.' No half measures. I remember once venturing the suggestion that some persons with whom the two of us happened to be at variance were blinkered. 'Blinkered!' he replied with unutterable scorn. This was the secret of his success as a publisher: 'They think,' he said of some publishing associates intent on a take-over, 'that I'm just a toff. Well, I am a toff and that's how I run my business.' Never saying anything more or less than he thought: it was not a bad recipe, though it made it impossible for him to go on television and his lawyers were afraid of his talking to journalists. But positive things too, and friendship itself, were expressed without reserve and there was a warm, Mediterranean side to him in any life crisis. The many who came to Ely Place for his funeral loved all these qualities and found it hard to believe at the gathering afterwards that he was not, as usual, laughing uproariously, in a corner and yet somehow at the centre of the party. For his friends he still fills (in Johnson's marvellously ambiguous words) affection's eye.

George Weidenfeld

At Weidenfeld & Nicolson

The seven years of my collaboration with Colin Haycraft belong to the most exciting and gratifying experiences of my working life. As the editor of the World University Library, a range of eighty books published in a dozen languages and including some outstanding works, he turned a fuzzy, abstract brief (mine) for a schematic, encyclopaedic series into a pragmatic, earthy, yet intellectually distinguished, highly individualistic, coherent list.

He was a stubborn perfectionist when it came to quality; he was merciless in his criticism and unimpressed by mandarins. He affected a stoical manner but he could be passionate, sometimes despairing, but never lacking in humour, even if it was *galgenhumor* on occasions when he felt that an author let us down. One of his great successes was Richard Gregory's *Eye and Brain* which, with its lively graphics complementing an admirably concise text, heralded a new style of publishing.

Although he liked to think of himself – and was – quintessentially English, he proved himself an excellent and canny 'internationalist' in mediating between a dozen, sometimes unruly, foreign publishers, always winning their respect and trust. I was sorry when he left to run his own business and have always admired what he achieved and what he attempted to do. For me he was one of the last great humanists in British publishing.

Mervyn Horder

In the Hot Seat at Duckworth

Colin Haycraft's early publishing experience was as publicity man for The Bodley Head, then as editor of the World University Library for Weidenfeld & Nicolson. But his main feat was to hold down the hot seat at Duckworth for 25 years, maintaining that distinguished small firm as a distinguished small firm throughout. He believed almost mystically, as well as pragmatically, in the advantages of a firm producing and distributing its own books in the heart of London, its staff working the whole day in the middle of their own book stock.

He never took a holiday and could seldom even be tempted to leave Camden Town, where his home, his books and his office all were; but he might occasionally be found upstairs on his bed reading Plutarch in the Greek. Classical scholarship of the most rigorous kind was both his refuge and relaxation. In 25 years of bandying Greek and Latin scraps with him, I only once caught him out, and that in a matter of a single Greek letter: ἁ γέγραφα γέγραφα, he said one day, and I knew that ἁ should be ὁ. And even Colin across the years never found for me the author of the hexameter quoted in *Brewer's Dictionary of Phrase & Fable*:

> Cattus amat pisces, sed non vult tingere plantas.

I saw in him the scholar of Frances Cornford's poem:

> With us you seemed
> A quiet happy sailor come of late
> From those strange seas you best could navigate,
> knowing a world that others only dreamed.

By temperament he was disposed, after his own early achievements, to despise lesser mortals: you had to give him evidence of merit or exceptional qualification before he began to respect you. A special scorn was reserved for Americans and for literary women – this last barrier successfully crashed by two persons only, his wife, the novelist Alice Thomas Ellis, and Beryl Bainbridge, both of whose works contributed largely to keeping his firm afloat.

By temperament too, Haycraft was fanatical about copy preparation and proof-reading, and though he had competent and devoted editorial assistance he could hardly bear not to do all the work himself.

Finance was another story. While he knew good net profit when he saw it, he was incapable of the eternal niggling vigilance necessary to secure it for a small firm. Better now draw a veil across the many errors of judgement, big and small, that required his Duckworth operation to be rescued by three successive monied knights-errant, each time in a crescendo of acrimony.

It must be remembered that when they bought control of Duckworth in 1968, Haycraft was in harness with Tim Simon (son of the Curwen Press Oliver Simon), whose function it was to provide, as he was qualified to, both the finance and the financial wisdom to get their joint enterprise started. But by Tim's death in New York two years later Haycraft was left to carry on by himself without either of Tim's contributions and without any inbuilt flair for the manipulation of money. His charm and quick thinking persuaded a few, but by no means all, authors that to be published by Duckworth was glory enough and that the money did not matter so much.

Of one publishing innovation he was quietly proud. Amid the howls from the trade which greet most innovations, he led the way in 1979 in the pricing up of scholarly works of limited appeal. M.A. Screech's *Rabelais* (300 pages), was issued at £33 net instead of the £18.50 usual at the time. (Looking into the figures a year later we found that though sales had been fewer than hoped, the net receipts of both author and publisher were very slightly better than expected.) Now everybody is doing it.

'By their fruits ye shall know them.' A list with active books on it by Richard Gregory, Kenneth Dover, John Passmore, John Steane, Ernst Gombrich, Donald West, Michael Dummett, Brian McGuinness, Oliver Sacks, Hugh Lloyd-Jones, John Symonds and Richard Mullen not only needs no bush, but neatly reveals both the bent of Haycraft's mind and the level of his brow.

Haycraft may take his place with the best of the strongly individualist publishers of the century: Grant Richards, Martin Secker, Leonard Woolf, Hamish Hamilton, Rupert Hart-Davis, Nash, Dobson, Calder, Owen and the rest: with this difference, that all the others sought to live by exercising their discrimination in matters literary.

Haycraft saw early that British literature is for the present in the doldrums, the proliferation of literary prizes merely serving to flog a dying horse (and who shall gainsay him about that?), and so went out to battle in the up-and-coming popular-academic field, where his one-man band was often able to provide – sometimes with the help of a hefty subsidy – a prompter, more personal service than could orthodox university presses or over-staffed general publishers with all their marketing gimmicks.

His wit was legendary, and instant. If there is room to preserve one example here, let it be his reply to someone who asked him why, since his heroes were Erasmus and Gibbon, he didn't write more himself. 'Who wants a pregnant midwife anyway?'

Most of those who worked for him at Duckworth stayed there many years. All those of us who cherished him for his urchin charm and his solid achievements – however maddened we were by some of his other traits – will be finding North London a poorer place with him no longer round the corner there.

Beryl Bainbridge

Mr Chips

Now that Colin Haycraft, that brilliant, life-enhancing, often infuriating man, is dead, what was it that made him so important to those of us who were privileged to count him as a friend? We will each remember him differently – he was not someone who was all things to all men – save in his talent for friendship and an intuitive, almost feminine capacity for understanding the nature of others.

I first met him through his wife, the novelist Alice Thomas Ellis. One afternoon in 1970, our children attending the same school, she telephoned to ask me if her son and mine were playing out in the street. I said hers had just gone home. 'Just a minute,' she said, perhaps recognising the Liverpool accent in my voice, 'what was your maiden name?' It transpired we had met twenty years before, up north, in the house of a mutual friend. She said she'd read two of my novels, both of which she thought promising in spite of verbosity; in those days I scattered adjectives like autumn leaves. Had I written anything else? As it happened, I had, a first book considered too obscene to print by every publishing house in London. I was invited to bring my dog-eared manuscript round to her house in Gloucester Crescent; and that was the beginning of my career as a writer. Without Anna Haycraft, alias Alice Thomas Ellis, I doubt if I would have gone on writing.

I'm not sure that Colin ever read that early book; he didn't think much of fiction, not unless it had been written by someone like Fielding. This unconventional attitude was surprisingly helpful to the aspiring writer. If Colin, after a cursory glance at an opening chapter, could neither follow the story nor remember the name of the hero, it meant one had fallen at the first hurdle. His method was simple. If a bottom line read, 'Singing, George walked down the road,' followed by a turn of the page and a sentence beginning, 'He was feeling out of sorts', Colin would immediately ask, 'Who was out of sorts?' It was useless to point out that it was obviously George; if Colin hadn't caught on, nobody else would.

It was he who gave me the idea for my novel, *Watson's Apology*, a fictional reconstruction of a real murder committed in 1871 by an elderly clergyman who had been for many years headmaster of Stockwell Grammar School. Browsing, as was his habit, through the *Dictionary of National Biography*, Colin came across the entry, John Selby Watson, author and murderer. Left to myself, I might have made the whole thing up, but Colin's passion for accuracy led to an orgy of research which occupied two years. This in itself was of immense value to me. Having left school at fourteen, I had little knowledge of Greek, Latin, History, the Education Act, the legal and penal system or life in London in the 19th century, all of which was fairly necessary if I was to portray the life of a scholar, a headmaster and a convicted murderer. I didn't even know how to use the catalogues in the London Library, a deficiency only partially rectified by Colin in a teaching seminar which started in a nearby pub and ended on the landing outside the reading room; I passed out cold on a convenient sofa.

In pursuit of Watson's past we tracked down the resting place of his butchered wife in Tooting Bec cemetery. At no time did Colin have any sympathy for the battered Mrs W. Ever the publisher, he would groan, 'What a tragedy! All the poor chap wanted to do was get on with his *Life of the Popes*.' The gates were locked when we arrived – dusk, as they say, was falling – but I managed to jump over the railings and find a ladder for Colin to descend. Athletic as he was, being a chap he was sensibly cautious of hurdling spikes. 'One foot in the grave,' he muttered, as he clambered into the grounds. We didn't know that we'd been spotted by a caretaker/grave-digger who had promptly rung the police with the information that two teenagers, possibly members of a witchcraft circle (we were spied from a distance and were both small in stature) had illegally entered the cemetery. Faced with officers of the law Colin became uncharacteristically apologetic – he'd dispute this, of course – and rambled on about his being a director of Duckworth's. Knowing that very few people, let alone the police, read books, I tried to say that we were just looking for a murdered wife, but Colin gave me such a withering glance that I shut up. It was the only time I felt I knew more about people than he did.

Though it was true that he was best known as a distinguished publisher, he was first and foremost a teacher of considerable power, when least intended. Though sometimes acerbic with equals he never spoke down to those less educated than himself. This could be bewildering, as when he told one of his jokes in a dead tongue and expected his listener to be tickled by it as much as he was; but he had a God-given gift for making one feel capable of discussing, with a little prodding and a little judicious reading, such weighty matters as the causes of the Peloponnesian Wars, the continuing reverberations of the French Revolution, the drinking habits of Porson and Dr Johnson, or the astonishing dilemma of Fatty Arbuckle, whose weight, during sexual congress, ruptured the liver of a starlet and caused her unfortunate death.

His more formal tutoring was a shade less successful. Two years before he died he offered to teach me and three little boys, two of whom were my grandsons, the rudiments of Latin. Every Saturday morning we sat before him round the table in the basement and struggled to master declensions and substantives. If the Belgians weren't oppugnabant(ing) the reverse was happening with the Cotta, 'Cotta Belgas oppugnaverat'. The Barbarians came into it somewhere. Colin fired his questions so brusquely and expected such immediate replies that he invariably answered them himself. The little boys soon learned that an innocent enquiry as to what was meant by the Ides of March or the derivation of the word 'barbarian' could deflect Mr Chips into delivering a lecture which took up the entire lesson.

It is not generally known that Colin wrote the prefaces to *Natural Baby Food* and *The Sayings of Dr Johnson* under the pseudonym of Brenda O'Casey. For the former work a photograph was required for the jacket, and Colin duly appeared, fetchingly attired in a tweed skirt and auburn wig. Alas, that vision of the chairman of Duckworth, glasses glinting on his snub nose, hairless legs encased in lisle stockings, was never captured. The photographer, helpless with laughter, forgot to insert a film. At the launch of *Natural Baby Food*, the press, alerted to the arrival of Miss O'Casey, was informed that she had been arrested on her journey from Scotland after an inebriated affray on the express from Edinburgh.

Two weeks after my initial visit to the Haycrafts' house, I sat cross-legged on the drawing-room floor – in those days, one did that sort of thing in Camden Town – and somewhat impertinently asked Colin why he seemed so happy. He had a very characteristic sitting position, one suede-shoed foot swinging up and down, bow-tie only slightly askew, mannikin cigar held between third and fourth finger, second finger stabbing the air to emphasise a point. 'Happiness', he said, 'is being able to pay one's bills.'

It is ironic, cruel, that in the end it was this particular inability that struck him down. In the early 1990s the firm needed capital and took on investors, with whom he quickly fell out. This debacle led to a board meeting in which he was given two hours to clear his desk. The locks to the Duckworth premises were changed after he went home that evening. Not one to be dismissed so peremptorily, he gathered his forces, marshalled his friends and went into battle. Less than a fortnight later an extraordinary meeting – now always referred to as the Boardroom Coup – was held in the offices of Stephen Hill, financier and lover of the classics. The decision of the investors was overturned, and Colin restored behind the manuscripts piled upon his desk. Sadly, the fight to win complete control of the firm lasted nearly two years, in the course of which his health deteriorated and his zest for combat flagged.

Once this demoralising process had begun, the end came swiftly. It was not so much that he was defeated, rather that he was bored with having to expend his energies tilting at lawyers and accountants.

How can one sum him up? Perhaps by the words he himself used of Dr Johnson, partly taken from Boswell:

The appeal of [his] character lies in the remarkable union of robust common sense with true tenderness of heart ... He despised people who 'talked from books', and he judged books by the same standard as he judged people, affectation being the worst crime in both ... Since [his] prejudices are so often the right ones, or at any rate acceptable ones, we generally succumb to the sense, while always admiring the force and humour of what he says ... [He] regarded conversation as a social contest ... 'He was sometimes jocular, but you felt as if you were playing with a lion's paw ... he had a heavy look, but when he spoke it was like lightning out of a dark cloud' ... His very prejudices were always displayed with wit or educated insolence.

'Quite!', as Colin would say, tapping off the ash on his cigar and looking down with assumed innocence.

Forget Dr Johnson. I loved him.

Oliver Sacks

Midwife and Unmuddler

I first saw Colin in 1951, when I was a freshman at Queen's. He was in his final year – a short, energetic figure, in his scholar's gown, already slightly Gibbonian in confidence and mannerism, but very agile and darting in movement, and said to be a brilliant rackets-player as well as a classical scholar. But we did not speak, did not meet, until 20 years later.

I had written the first nine case-histories of *Awakenings* in the summer of 1969, but this had been turned down (as well as two other quasi-books written that summer) by Faber & Faber, a rejection which threw me, and made me wonder if I would ever complete or publish a book again. Raymond Greene, of Heinemann, who had reviewed my first book, *Migraine*, warmly when it came out at the start of 1971, wanted to commission me to write a book on Parkinsonism 'just like it'. This both encouraged me and discouraged me, because I did not want to repeat myself; I felt a quite different sort of book was called for, but I had no idea *what* sort of book it should be.

My old friend Jonathan Miller, who lived across the road from Colin, seeing my quandary, wandered over to him at the end of '71 and gave him a carbon copy of *Awakenings* – at least, of the nine case histories I had written in 1969, but which, discouraged and uncertain, I had never added to.

Colin was excited by the histories, said I should publish them, urged me to write more. This, in turn, excited me, but scared me too. Colin pressed, gently; I demurred; he drew back, waited, moved in once again – he was very sensitive, very delicate, with my diffidence, my anxieties. I prevaricated for six months. The first letter of mine I can find in my huge file of our correspondence dates from June 2, 1972:

> Dear Mr Haycraft,
> I have been infernally rude in keeping silent for so long. This is partly because I have had to struggle with absurd compunctions about publishing detailed case histories, partly because I have been uncertain about how to organize the (often tragic) 'follow-ups' of the patients ...
> I think I have now sorted out what to say, and squared it with my conscience, and I feel ready, finally, to get started.

I have elsewhere written about the more personal influences on *Awakenings* – without, I fear, giving Colin his due; for if it had not been for him, *Awakenings*, I think, would never have been finished, much less published. Most crucial, perhaps, was his sudden decision to put the nine histories I gave him *in proof* – he did this without warning, in July '72, in the impulsive-intuitive way he often did things. It was a most generous, not to say extravagant act – what guarantee had he that I would ever continue my writing? – and, also, a crucial act of faith. It convinced me, more than any words could, that he was in earnest, that he was not just talking, that he *really* thought *Awakenings* should be published.

This decided me. I got a flat in Hampstead within easy reach of the Old Piano Factory in Gloucester Crescent, secured myself a shorthand typist (I had a neck injury at the time, with such wasting of the right hand I could not hold a pen), and forced myself to work and dictate daily – a forcing which rapidly became a delight as I got into the work more and more. Almost every day I sent completed bunches of typescript down to Colin, which we would then go over in minute detail. We spent hours, that summer, closeted together.

And yet I see, from letters between us, that we still preserved a considerable formality: he was always 'Mr Haycraft', I was always 'Dr Sacks':

August 30, 1972
12 Redington Rd.

Dear Mr Haycraft,

I enclose, herewith, five more case histories. The sixteen
histories thus far run about 240 pages in aggregate, which
would be between 50 and 60,000 words ... I am thinking of
adding four further ones ... (I added details) – but I will
defer here, of course, to your judgement in the matter.

... I have tried to move from piles and compilations of
medical lists to *stories*, but obviously without complete
success. You're so right about the shape of Art and the
shapelessness of Life – perhaps I should have had a keener,
cleaner line or theme in them all, but they are so complex,
like tapestries. To some extent these are crude ore, which
others (including myself) can dig in and refine later.

With kindest regards

September 7

Dear Mr Haycraft,

I have spent several days on an introduction ... which I
herewith enclose. I only seem to find the right way after
making every possible blunder, and finally exhausting all
the wrong ways ... I need to talk to you again soon ... as
always, because you help me to unmuddle ...

But it was not just unmuddling that I demanded of Colin at
this time, it was emotional support, when I was blocked, or when
my mood and confidence sagged, as they did, almost to the point
of collapse, after the first rush was over:

19th Sept.

Dear Mr Haycraft,

I seem to be in one of those dry, dead depressed phases
where one can only do nothing or blunder round in circles.
The damn thing is that it needs only three days good work
to finish the book, but I don't know whether I am capable of
this at the moment.

I am in such an uneasy, guilt-stricken mood at the moment that I think I can't bear the thought of any of my

patients being recognizably exposed, or the hospital itself
being recognized in *Awakenings* – maybe this is one of the
things which is inhibiting me from finishing the book ...

My moods too Colin unmuddled and soothed, along with all
the intricate, convoluted, sometimes labyrinthine ins and outs of
the book, so that by November it was finally finished. In the final
month of writing – I was in a state of great grief, my mother had
just died – I more or less moved to the Old Piano Factory, and
Colin became a mother for me as well as a midwife. The impulse
to destroy was so great at this time that Colin and I agreed I
should slip each page under the door of his office as it was
written. When the book was published, I expressed my gratitude
to him for his 'delicate and profound maieuticê technê' – but it
was not just critical acumen and midwifery that he provided, but
a sense of shelter and support, finally almost a home, which I
needed quite as much at the time.

But perhaps it was only when the book was on its way that we
could both relax into a more personal mode, and that we started
to move from the relation of publisher and writer to that of being
friends as well. I started to visit Colin at his home at this time,
and to meet some of his friends and the rest of his family. His
high, book-filled Victorian house, at 22 Gloucester Crescent, was
just a two-minute walk from the Old Piano Factory, and Colin
spent his waking life in either place, indifferently. There seemed
no very clear division between working and home life, and if 22
itself was filled with authors and manuscripts – much of the
essential editorial work was done at the kitchen table, while
Anna, placid, cooked on her Aga – the atmosphere of the Factory,
at number 43, with its vast 22-sided main room, and its angular
corridors, and Colin's own office with its untidy piles of books,
was also somehow domestic and homey. In fine weather, conversation, and work, would move outside, to the little ferny garden
in front of 22; and at lunchtime, to the garden of the Edinburgh
Castle, the local pub.

In October of 1972 I first met Richard Gregory (whom I considered not only a genius, but the most human and idiosyncratic
figure in the contemporary scientific scene) in Colin's crowded,

cranky office; they were, it turned out, very old friends, and Colin was to publish *Illusion in Nature and Art*, edited by Richard and Ernst Gombrich in 1973, and Richard's huge volume of collected papers, *Concepts and Mechanisms of Perception*, the following year. Over the years I was to meet many of Colin's other authors and friends (many of his authors later became his friends) – at the Factory, or his home, or both.

His friends, like his authors and books, were typical of the wide range and catholic tastes of Colin's own keen and sceptical, but also warm and generous, mind. He had loved the classics since childhood, and enjoyed composing Greek and Latin epigrams in his bath as a relaxation – he made the Duckworth classics list, which had been languishing before he took over, into the most distinguished in the country. But he was also one of the first publishers, if not the first, to see the importance of computers – whether as practical devices, or as possible analogues and allies of the human mind – and he brought out a novel computer list early in the '80s (very startling, and original, and prescient, at the time). He would follow any lead, any impulse, with the greatest pertinacity. Having decided (despite his atheism) that St Jerome was of great importance, and observing that there had never been a biography of him, he hunted down the only man in England (possibly the planet) who knew anything about him, and wooed him patiently for years until he produced a biography.

Other publishers might have a dozen different editors, each with a particular speciality. Duckworth had only Colin, but Colin was so versatile, so spacious mentally, that he could grasp the central thought and intention of each of his authors, and then bring his own active powers to bear, and work on the book, work on the author, until he had achieved for it the greatest possible clarity and beauty. Such an entering-into, at once sympathetic and critical, I never felt as intrusive; I felt, rather, that I had been guided to *myself*, to defining more exactly, what I need and wanted to say – and equally, what I should be at pains not to say. Richard Gregory writes in his prescript to *Odd Perceptions* of how Colin 'looked through the essays, and as usual gave the best of advice, sometimes including, "Don't!" ' Colin's 'Don'ts!' were, indeed, as important as his 'Do's', and saved me, at least some of the time, from the lapses, the aberrations, the failures of intelligence and taste, we are all prone to.

Odd coincidences brought Colin and me together. We were both extremely fond of the eighteenth century and its quintessential figures – Pope, Hume, Gibbon, Boswell, Johnson (Gibbon's irony was particularly to Colin's taste, as was Hume's scepticism and atheism). Pope and Gibbon had already made their appearance in *Migraine*, but it was Colin who suggested a passage from Boswell for *Awakenings* (Boswell: 'How does poor Smart do, Sir? Is he likely to recover?' Johnson: 'It seems as if his mind has ceased to struggle with the disease; for he grows fat upon it.'). Colin later encouraged the introduction of Johnson into *A Leg to Stand On* – where he is invoked to kick out a Berkeleyan phantom – and of Hume, repeatedly, in *The Man Who Mistook His Wife For a Hat*. Colin was also drawn to Leibniz, as I was – he had published Ishiguro's edition of Leibniz's *Philosophy of Logic and Language* in 1972; and introduced me in '73 to John Hostler, whose book, *Leibniz' Moral Philosophy*, he was to publish a couple of years later; and encouraged me to be free with Leibniz references in *Awakenings*.

But also, unlike Colin, I had at this time a certain religious hunger; and it was partly this which drew me to Anna too, and to have with her a different sort of relation, on a more emotional, more religious, less rationalistic basis. It was with her that I corresponded most intensely after the death of my mother in 1972, and of her son Joshua in 1978.

In November of '72, after finishing the manuscript of *Awakenings* ('You're not to *touch* it again!' Colin had said when I slipped him the last page), I was invited to the Haycraft house for Sunday dinner. All went well, until Anna suddenly said sharply, 'WIPE YOUR MOUTH, Oliver!' I wiped my mouth guiltily, feeling like a dirty little boy of 10. Then I realised that this was, in fact, addressed to a dirty little boy of 10 who bore the same name as myself. Strangely, I had never met another Oliver before, and nor had Oliver Haycraft.

Galley proofs of *Awakenings* were produced early in 1973, and I gave Auden a set when I visited him in Oxford in February (he was the only other person to see them beside Colin and myself).

Page proofs came a couple of months later, but I was never sent
these, because Colin was afraid that I would seize the opportunity to make innumerable changes and additions, as I had done
with the galleys, and delay the scheduled publication.[1] But when
Colin, on the other hand, suggested postponing publication, so
that sections could be prepublished in the *Sunday Times*, I was
strongly against this, because I now had a most urgent desire to
see the book out, and, crucially, on or before my birthday in July.
I would be forty then, and I wanted to be able to feel I had now
blown my life entirely, to be able to say, 'I may be forty, I have
lost my youth, but at least I have done something, I have written
this book.' Colin thought I was being irrational, but seeing my
state of mind, he agreed to restore the original publication date
in late June. (He later recollected that Gibbon had been at pains
to publish the final volume of the *History* on *his* birthday.)

Colin gave a grand party in his house just before publication
day – a party I think I enjoyed more than any in my life, because
it was not only a party for the birth of the book, but in effect a
'coming out' party for a new, more public me. From now on, for
better or worse, I would no longer be a wholly private person,
known only to my patients, a few friends, my family – there
would be a second, public identity, as the author of *Awakenings*.
I had scarcely had this feeling with *Migraine*, a necessarily more
modest and limited book.

Colin adored parties and was a consummate host, somehow
managing to talk to everybody (even in the largest gatherings)
as if they were the only one, at least the only interesting one,
there. And though (to my somewhat frugal taste) there was far
too much liquor at his parties, and everybody (Colin included)
got a bit tipsy, this only heightened their sense of intimacy and
geniality.

I had missed the Duckworth Christmas party at the end of

---

[1] Indeed, within days of my leaving the completed ms. with Colin, I could only
think of what I had omitted from the book. In something of a frenzy, feeling like
the little boy of Vollendam, I started to plug its apertures, its omissions (as I saw
them) with footnotes. Now back in New York, I sent these, almost daily, by
special messenger to Colin. Colin seemed to like these, but finally he exploded:
'They come, in aggregate, to three times the length of the book.' Colin said I could
keep twelve (later he relented, and let me keep eighty-two) and one he himself
inserted, a pun on Godness, goodness and Guinness.

1972, but from now on I made a point of attending every one, as well as the other, special parties which Colin loved giving ... and there were to be many such over the years. One, on Saturday, 27th June, 1987, was 'to celebrate the 200th anniversary of the completion of *The History of the Decline and Fall of the Roman Empire*', and the invitation card was embossed with Gibbon's famous words: 'It was on the day, or rather night, of the 27th of June, 1787, between the hours of eleven and twelve, that I wrote the last lines of the last page, in a summer house in my garden...'

Another, in 1990, at Johnson's House in Gough Square, was a special party 'to celebrate publication of *The Sayings of Dr Johnson* [and *The Sayings of Lord Byron*][2] '. Since Colin (and most of his friends) were chain smokers, it was added on the invitation, 'We regret that for insurance reasons there can be no smoking.' But Colin, characteristically, had sweetened the prohibition with a charming quote from Johnson:

> Smoking has gone out. To be sure, it is a shocking thing, blowing smoke out our mouths into other people's mouths, eyes, and noses, and having the same thing done to us. Yet I cannot account, why a thing which requires so little exertion, and yet preserves the mind from total vacuity, should have gone out. Every man has something by which he calms himself: beating with his feet, or so.

Anything to do with Gibbon or Johnson scholarship excited and delighted Colin – and as he had given these special parties for his heroes (actually he disliked the word, the inflationary concept of 'hero', and Gibbon and Johnson, if anything, were his favourite anti-heroes – heroes of irony and deflation) so he made one of his own rather rare ventures into newsprint the same year, when a facsimile edition of Johnson's *Dictionary* was brought out ('only 235 years' after the original), in a characteristically brilliant and quirky piece in *The Observer*, coupled with an appeal to keep Johnson's house going.

Colin loved the *Dictionary*, and virtually knew it by heart, not

---

[2] The latter was 'for the women' Colin said in a witty speech on this occasion, rationalising an uncharacteristically Romantic departure cajoled out of him by the book's editor. (ed.)

just the words, but the characteristically witty and often sardonic definitions. And on the rare occasions when he let himself go, in letters, he could raise an artillery of Johnsonian magniloquence, as in one letter where, speaking of an eminent dramatist, he decries 'all his grunts and groans and pseudo-profundities and bursts of fatuous aposiopesis'.

With *Awakenings* published, I could turn to other things. I had been interested in Tourette's syndrome for several years, ever since some of my 'Awakenings' patients had become Tourettic on L-DOPA; and this, indeed, had been the subject of one of the half-written books rejected (along with *Awakenings*) by Faber in 1969, and now Colin encouraged me to consider a whole book on the subject. Returning to New York after *Awakenings* was published, I decided to work in a back ward of a state psychiatric hospital, exploring autism, retardation and childhood psychosis – and here too we had the feeling that a book might come of this. But, in the event, neither of these came about. The actual subject of the next book was (to put it mildly) of an unanticipated sort – my tangle with a bull on a mountain in Norway, my ending up as an orthopaedic patient in London.

Colin was alarmed when he heard of my accident, but fascinated when I told him how it happened and what was going on with me in the hospital. 'This is grand stuff!' he exclaimed. 'You have to write all about it ...' He paused, then added, curiously, 'It sounds as if you're actually living the book now.' A few days later, he brought me along an enormous dummy of a book he had just published (a dummy, as it happened, of Michael Dummett's book on Frege) – seven hundred empty, creamy white pages, so that I could make full notes and observations as I lay in my room. I was delighted with this huge dummy, the largest notebook I had ever had, and kept the fullest notes of my own involuntary journey, as I saw it, into the no-man's land of total non-experi-ence. (Other patients, later, seeing me with this huge book, would say, 'Ah, you lucky bugger – we just go through it, but you're making a book of it all.') Colin called frequently, to check up on my progress – this, for him, was the progress of my observations, of my 'book', quite as much as my progress as a patient – and Anna too came, with fruit and trout and poetry and what-not, in a less agendous mode.

By May of 1975 I had written a rough draft of *Leg* – it was Jonathan Miller who suggested the title *A Leg to Stand On* – and considered (as Colin did) that it could soon be polished and readied for publication. Colin was so confident, indeed, that he included it in his upcoming 1976-77 catalogue. But in the event, *A Leg to Stand On* was not to be published in 1977, or '78, or '79, or '80; nor in '81, or '82, or '83. Most of my friends thought it would never be published.

There were problems with this book of a sort I had not had before, because writing it involved reliving the experience, reliving the passivity and horrors of patienthood; involved too an exposure of myself, and of my own intimate feelings, in a way which my more 'doctorly' writings never involved.

And something went wrong between Colin and me that summer, of 1975, as I strove to finish the book. The Millers went up to Scotland in August, and allowed me the use of their house. This was right opposite Colin's house, as close as one could get – what could be more ideal for the work that lay ahead?

But the proximity which had been so delightful, so productive, with *Awakenings*, now unhappily had the opposite effect. I would write every morning, spend the afternoon walking, swimming, and every evening, around 7 or 8, Colin would come by. He had eaten by then, had usually drunk a good deal too, and tended, more often than not, to be flushed, irritable and argumentative. The August nights were hot and airless, and perhaps there was something about my manuscript, or something about me, which brought out his anger – I was tense and anxious that summer, and uncertain about my writing. He would pick one of the pages I had typed, read a sentence or a paragraph, and then attack it – its tone, its style, its substance, its everything. He would take each sentence, each thought and worry it to death – or so it seemed to me. He showed, I thought, none of the humour, the geniality, I had expanded in before, but a censoriousness so strict I shrivelled before it. After these evening sessions, I would have an impulse to tear up the day's work, to feel the book was idiocy, that I could or should not go on.

The summer of '75 ended on an evil note, and (though I never encountered Colin in such a state ever again) it cast a shadow on the years to come. Thus *Leg* was not, after all, completed that year.

Many versions of *Leg* were to be written over the next few years, each longer, more intricate, more labyrinthine than the last. Even the letters I sent to Colin were of inordinate length – one, from 1978, ran to more than 5,000 words, with a brief addendum of another 2,000.

Finally, at the start of 1983, I was able to send a huge, though coherent, manuscript off to him – each section of the book, neatly typed, was on paper of a different colour, though the whole manuscript was now over 300,000 words.

Colin was infuriated by the sheer size of the manuscript, its obsessive poundings and reiterations of certain themes. But also he hesitated to cut, and often quoted Gibbon, and the fear he expressed, that in pruning his own work, he would eradicate some choice flowers along with the weeds. His choice was, rather, to make me re-write, re-express myself in more succinct form. The editing of *Leg*, unlike that of *Awakenings*, was immensely time-consuming (it took virtually the whole of '83), as well as being a strain on us both. The final version, after cutting and re-writing, was reduced to less than a fifth of the original size, a mere 58,000 words. The book appeared, seven years after it was slated, in May 1984.

The final re-writing was done in January 1984, and it was with a sense of great relief that I now relinquished the whole book to him. I had never been able to rid myself of a superstitious feeling that my 1974 accident was waiting to re-happen, and that it would re-happen, indeed, if I did not exorcise it by venting the entire thing in a book. Now it was out, now it was done – I was in no more danger of recapitulating the whole thing. But the unconscious is wilier than we realise, and ten days later – it was an icy day in the Bronx – I managed to fall in a particularly clumsy way, and so indeed to bring about the re-accident I so feared. When I called Colin from my hospital bed, he said, 'Ah, Oliver – you'd do anything for a footnote!'

After the heights and depths we had been through with *Awakenings* and *Leg*, our relationship became lighter and easier. If the year-long editing of *Leg* had almost killed us both, working together on the *Hat* book, as we both called it, was straightforward – though it lacked the intensity of our work, our collaboration, on *Leg* and *Awakenings*. Many of the pieces in *Hat* had already been published, and Colin, besides editing the rest, suggested how they might be divided into four groups, with introductions and interconnections for each of these. He helped turn the book from a collection of separate pieces to a unified whole. The book was published very swiftly, in November 1985, just six months after the manuscript was completed.

Over the years, it seems to me, there was hardly a subject under the sun I didn't talk about with Colin. He was a brilliant, irreverent, often outrageous talker, who loved to tease and adopt untenable positions out of sheer perverseness, or for the sheer joy of provoking an argument, an intellectual combat. It was playfulness, lightfootedness, intellectual repartee, wit, that he excelled and delighted in most of all – as he had, physically, in his youth, in his rackets-playing days. Colin was opinionated, to an extraordinary degree; but unlike many opinionated people, he was happy to expose his opinions to debate, and – if convinced that he was in error – to revise them entirely. He might say, with E.M. Forster, 'I do not believe in Belief', and for this reason he could never be a church man or party man, an institutional man of any sort. But beneath his playfulness, his irony, his sarcasms, his scorns, he had a passionate, defiant belief in the sanctity of the individual, and of the need, first and last, to be true to one's nature.

There was no one in the publishing world at all comparable to him, in his unremitting love of the classics, and of quality; or in his brilliance, his argumentativeness, his pigheadedness, his sweetness. Colin was never moved by profit or profitability, and intellectual and moral probity made Duckworth unique among publishers, able to maintain the highest quality in a declining, venal world.

But it was exactly this uncompromising purity of motive and value which hit Duckworth, hit Colin, most cruelly in the 1990s, as he struggled to maintain his autonomy and Duckworth's in a publishing world increasingly given over to profit and big business.

The last time I saw Colin was at Richard Gregory's seventieth birthday party in August '93. I met up with Beryl Bainbridge – she was perhaps Colin's and Anna's closest friend, and lived just round the corner from them (and I had known her too since '72) – and together we picked up Colin and took the train to Bristol, where Richard was having a grand party in his Exploratory. Colin looked thinner and better than I had seen him in years, though at first perhaps slightly subdued. But he seemed wholly recovered from the small stroke he had had – neither my neurological nor my friend's eye could detect anything amiss – and, as we neared Bristol, he became his old, cocky, rambunctious self.

He loved the party, and talked to everybody, and then gave a graceful and brilliant birthday speech for Richard, full of classical allusion, rationalism, misogyny, opinionation, as well as a deep and loving appreciation of his old friend. It was vintage Colin, at his full, outrageous best. I am glad that this is my last memory of him.

Hugh Lloyd-Jones

Publisher of the Ancient Classics

I first got to know Colin Haycraft while he was working for Weidenfeld & Nicolson. It was then that he suggested that I should edit for him the series *Classical Life and Letters*; he remembered old series, such as *Heroes of the Nations* and *English Men of Letters*, long edited by John Morley. Then together with Tim Simon he bought Duckworth from Mervyn Horder, and contrived to take the series with him. From that time I was a regular visitor to the old premises near Covent Garden, memorably described by Anthony Powell in *What's Become of Waring*, and later to the Old Piano Factory, so appropriate by reason of its unusual atmosphere and so conveniently located in Gloucester Crescent.

When he took over Duckworth I told him that I had worries about our having a formal business relationship, since we had become great friends; but he said that this would not matter, and it never did. Remembering that in the great days of the German classical periodical *Hermes*, the friends of Wilamowitz who were its editors, Friedrich Leo, Georg Kaibel and Carl Robert, did not simply wait for articles to be sent them but solicited them from the scholars whom they wished to publish, we invited certain scholars to contribute to the series; of those scholars who offered contributions some were accepted, but not all.

At that time the great university presses of England were publishing, as they had long been doing and still do, many valuable and learned works of classical scholarship. But though the persons in charge of their activities in this field had many admirable qualities, they were a little too like civil servants or the common run of academics, and they lacked dash and imagination. These qualities Colin had in abundance. His knowledge of and feeling for ancient literature was exceptional. He had done well in classics at The Queen's College, Oxford, of which he became an Honorary Fellow, and wrote Greek and Latin verse with ease and elegance. But with him classical scholarship was not simply an antiquarian hobby or a diverting kind of dilettantism; he had a strong sense of what the ancient world could teach us, and he had a flair for finding the scholars who were not only learned but alive.

At a certain stage the notion of a formal series was lost sight of; but he never ceased to publish works of classical scholarship, and few university presses had a list of such publications comparable with his. If I single out certain books, I realise that my choice is limited by my own restricted interests, and apologise to others; but the books that come immediately to mind, in alphabetical order, are J.N. Adams' *Latin Sexual Vocabulary*, Maurice Bowra's *Homer*, Anne Burnett's *Three Archaic Poets*, G.E.M. de Ste. Croix's *Origins of the Peloponnesian War* and *The Class Struggle in the Ancient Greek World*, Kenneth Dover's *Greek Homosexuality*, Jasper Griffin's *Latin Poets and Roman Life*, Leofranc Holford-Strevens' *Aulus Gellius*, Margaret Hubbard's *Propertius*, Edward Hussey's *The Presocratics*, Mary Lefkowitz's *Lives of the Greek Poets* and *Women in Greek Myth* and Mary Lefkowitz's and Maureen Fant's *Women's Life in Greece and Rome*, G.E.L. Owen's collected papers, Alessandro Perosa's and John Sparrow's *Renaissance Latin Verse*, Elizabeth Rawson's *Intellectual Life in the Late Roman Republic*, Donald Russell's *Plutarch*, D.R. Shackleton Bailey's *Cicero*, G.J. Toomer's translation of Ptolemy's *Almagest*, Alan Harris' translation of Wilamowitz's *History of Classical Scholarship*, Nigel Wilson's *Scholars of Byzantium* and (the latest) Netta Zagagi's *The Comedy of Menander*.

These titles are enough to show that it was a privilege to assist Colin in what he did for classical scholarship, but by themselves they do not suffice to give an idea of the immense pleasure of working with him. Publishers in general have a bad name with literary persons; in real life one thinks of the vile action of John Murray in destroying Byron's memoirs and in fiction of the trials experienced by Lucien de Rubempré in arranging for the publication of his novel *L'Archer de Charles Neuf*. One can imagine no person less like the image of a publisher suggested by such episodes than Colin Haycraft. One danger of a classical education, at least in England, is that many people who have had one are shamefully ignorant of other kinds of literature. Colin was far more cultivated than most dons, and with it all retained a youthful gaiety and insouciance. So far was he from the avarice and meanness popularly ascribed to members of his profession that he was careless about money matters to a fault. American authors tried hard to explain the importance of the American market and show him how to manage it, but to no purpose. Publishing with Colin was no way to make a fortune; but it was not in order to make money that one published with him.

No literary luncheons were like those at 22 Gloucester Crescent, with a variety of guests making lively conversation, while children came and went and the chaotic life of the house went on around one. London and Oxford literary gossip alternated with talk about books and about characters, ancient and modern. Colin was said by some people to be prejudiced against women writers and uninterested in fiction; but the most notable among the company were the two star novelists, Beryl Bainbridge and Alice Thomas Ellis. The latter would hover in the background, producing delicious food and not less delightful conversation; from the time when it was known that she was writing her first novel, everyone who knew her was certain that she would soon be famous, and so she was.

Colin's achievements will surely earn him a place in the cultural history of his period; and no one who knew him at all well is likely to forget him.

Alasdair MacIntyre

An Extended Conversation

Colin Haycraft's virtues as a publisher were no more and no other than his virtues as a human being – and among them were those qualities that would have led him to mock the first half of this sentence. No one was more suspicious of what he took to be sentimentality, and this perhaps just because of the genuine warmth of feeling that was so often masked by his irony. It would have been difficult to have been one of Duckworth's authors for any length of time without becoming one of Colin's friends, if only because he judged books and people by the same demanding standards. Among the qualities that he admired in both were wit, a love of scholarship, a hatred of the pretentious, the pedantic and the boring, an addiction to conversation and patience with outbursts of irascibility by others, including himself. He had immense confidence in his own judgments both about books and about people, and that confidence was surprisingly often justified. He was also an extraordinarily kind man.

He did of course have his blind spots. Within the whole range of classical studies he was at home to a degree that is very rare nowadays, even among classical scholars, and this in part because he was so completely at home in the classical languages. But with philosophy his touch was a little less sure. Contemporary philosophers were divided into three classes: those whom he admired and therefore published (the thought of publishing a philosopher whose work he did not admire was one that he could not have entertained), those whom he admired who were published by others (a class that ranged from Ryle and Ayer to David

Wiggins) and the unadmirable, unpublishable rest. No one gained entry to either of the first two classes who did not deserve it. But quite often philosophers just as admirable were consigned – sometimes on the basis, I suspect, of a very brief reading or some unfortunate encounter – to the third class. And once some-one was thus consigned, the sentence was permanent.

Colin and I were born on the same day, January 12, 1929, so sharing our birthdays with both Edmund Burke and Hermann Goering; and Colin charmed my mother by his curiosity about what she remembered of that day. But he and I did not meet until we were both in our late thirties, in Oxford in the period in which he was still working for Weidenfeld. By the time I had responded to his suggestion that I might want to collect together some of my essays, he had moved to, had in fact become Duck-worth. *Against the Self-Images of the Age*, from whose cover my face glowers out at the reader (Colin's joke), was the result. The joke was enhanced when Alfred Hitchcock took over Duckworth's then Covent Garden office as part of the setting for *Frenzy*, and a window filled with copies of my book was provided for Hitchcock's villain to glower back at, as he paused outside the front door.

When Duckworth moved to The Old Piano Factory in Gloucester Crescent, close to Colin's home, it became evident how much he was always the same person, wherever he was. Colin at home was of a piece with Colin at work and in both settings his dependence on Anna's wonderful combination of loving and hospitable generosity with unflinching objectivity was clear. The Haycraft household was one in which it was unusually difficult to avoid seeing things other than as they really are. I suffered from what was in Colin's eyes the consider-able disadvantage that, on matters about which he and Anna disagreed, I almost always took Anna to be in the right.

This was especially the case with questions of theology. When I first knew Colin, I was already impatient with dismissive attitudes to the claims of the Catholic church, as impatient as he was with anything other than just such a dismissive attitude. Our deep lack of sympathy with each other on this point turned out to be perhaps as important a component of our friendship as any of our agreements. Colin expended a very great deal of energy in fending off God. He thought it unfair and objectionable of me to suggest that no real unbeliever ever expends quite this amount of energy in this way. And so of course it was. But the vehemence of his response made it clear that the same thought haunted him.

From the time I emigrated to the United States in 1970, I had made a point of seeing Colin when I was in London, at least once each year. When I look back on these twenty-four years of conversations, I recognise that they were parts of one very long extended conversation, a conversation that has been among the great pleasures of my life. Colin excelled at conversation as much as he did at rackets or at writing Latin verse. So that I always looked forward eagerly to our next meeting. Oddly enough, I still do.

A.L. Rowse

*

The Scholar-Publisher

Alas, that I knew Colin so little – how much I wish that I had known him better, such a loss to us all, for he was a man of ideas – rare at any time – of initiative and drive (rarer still) – a real leader, and so a special loss to the world of publishing, and to us all.

He was that unusual bird, the scholar-publisher. They are few and far between. In the eighteenth century Dodsley was a poet of a sort, who himself collected the contemporary poets and published them in several volumes. In our time, Daniel and Harold Macmillan were good classical scholars at Balliol. As was Colin at Queen's. I wish I had known him then, only next door to All Souls. But in his years there I was away a good deal, in Cornwall and in America. So it happened that we knew each other only from correspondence in the last couple of years, and from his visit in the last months of his life to me, marooned on my Cornish headland.

From these contacts I could appreciate something of the remarkable, exceptional personality that his was – to which so many others who knew him better have paid tribute. He was above all – like people of the first rank and quality – an *encourager*, as I have found in my time and experience, with T.S. Eliot, G.M. Trevelyan, Sir John Neale. This is rarer than it should be in academic life. Trevelyan once said to me that he had the impression that his medievalists were 'looking over each other's shoulders'. My own phrase was that academics were apt to sting each other into frustration.

Not so Colin. I owed to him the books I wrote for him to his
suggestion. It was his idea that I should contribute to that
admirable series of people's characteristic sayings, the volume of
Shakespeare's. I'll bet the idea of that fascinating series sprang
from his fertile, literary mind. When I sent him my typescript,
he put in a lot of work all over it himself: it was obvious how
much he was interested and qualified to do the job on his own
lines. However, I made it clear that it was my book, and he took
that gallantly and well.

I had recently had a horrid experience. In New York publishing offices they will sometimes re-write an author's work for him.
In a review I had written about Christopher Marlowe in the *New
York Times Book Review*, an office boy, or editor, had actually
inserted a sentence I totally disagreed with, approving of the
erratic, indeed often crackpot, work of Leslie Hotson and
Frances Yates! The poor fellow didn't know what he was talking
about, and obviously didn't qualify to hold an opinion on Elizabethan scholarship. The simple rule should be the natural one:
the third rate should learn from the first rate, not the other way
round, reversing the order of nature.

Paul Johnson had a worse experience. An American publisher
tried to re-write his book for him. A tougher customer than I,
Paul told them straight that a publisher's business is to *publish*,
it is the writer's business to *write* the book, and withdrew his
book from them. The sheer impertinence of such people!

Colin was not an interferer, but he had an amusing vein of
obstinacy, which made me laugh as an obstinate man myself. I
had referred somewhere to Addison's Walk at Magdalen. Colin
would not have it to be – it was 'Addison Walk'. This involved
correspondence, for he would not take it from me: a conscientious
scholar, he had to telephone Magdalen and find that it was, of
course, Addison's. So he wrote me comically 'in sackcloth'. Actually it was fun for a Fellow of Queen's to slip up, for Addison had
been a Fellow of Queen's and made it his favourite walk, as it
had been mine. In the course of my long Oxford life, I must have
walked it ten times more often than either he or Colin had.

Swings and roundabouts – for, in return, I profited from
Colin's being a classical scholar to vet my rusty Latin. My
goodness, he had a sharp eye and was quick off the mark! I

suspect that he had exceptional powers of concentration. From the number of misprints a writer is confronted with today, evidently few people have – apart, of course, from the lower standards of education. As a good classicist, Colin knew all about that as well as I.

My book, *All Souls in my Time*, I owed entirely to Colin's suggestion. Unfortunately he insisted, against my wish, on including a List of Fellowship elections at the end. He procured the List from a casual librarian who took no trouble – and it was incomplete and incorrect. An aesthete, I wanted the book to conclude with the poems, which several people thought best in the book. I suspect that Colin was more practical-minded, and less of an aesthete. However, in future editions, that offending List should be omitted, in accordance with my wish.

Next thing, he had an idea for a book which I had not thought of, in spite of having written *Reflections on the Puritan Revolution* and – for him – *Four Caroline Portraits*. (He wanted to call it *Civil War Portraits*.) In those books, I paid my disrespects to the Philistine Puritans who were responsible for so much destruction in cathedrals and churches, sculpture, stained glass, brasses, tombs, fonts, organs, music; they dispersed the choirs, threw out one third of all the clergy. They shut down the stage, sold off the King's marvellous collection of pictures, threw the Queen's splendid Rubens altar-piece into the Thames, etc.

Since my fundamental values are aesthetic, I never forget the artistic losses the country suffered from that vile lot. Their descendants, the Politically Correct leftist academics, have no care for the arts and little visual sense, so they entirely overlook this side of things and spend their time on the nonsense they thought – Ranters, Soul-sleepers, Levellers, Muggletonians, fanatics and humbugs.

So these books of mine paid my disrespects to them on that score too. In fact much of my later work has been written in reaction to the silly, but dominant, tendencies of our squalid society today. Intelligent people agree now about the Silly Sixties, the Wilson Era of incessant strikes and superfluous immigration importing a problem we did not have before. Ironically enough, as I assured Colin, my views are much more in keeping with the consensus of intelligent opinion than those of the left intelligentsia are – a minority out of touch.

Colin, as an intelligent civilised man, understood all this, for he encouraged me to go on. He suggested that a book was wanting on the Regicides, the appalling culmination of decades of Puritan lying propaganda against King and Church. Again I had not thought of it, but I welcomed it as a further step in redressing the balance, against the pro-Puritan, pro-Parliament bias in the writing of our history since the Whig Macaulay. Even Macaulay's devoted nephew, George Macaulay Trevelyan, held the view that the terrible act of killing the King had the consequence of saving the monarchy in the long run. After the actual experience of the Puritan Revolution and the rule of the Saints, as they called themselves, the English people decided Never Again.

So my book on the Regicides depicts the ghastly record; the full significance of the Purge which made it possible has never been brought out in the text-books. I bring it out – I don't expect the Politically Correct to like that much. But what matter what the third-rate think? I am interested only in the work in and for itself. 'A fig for Opinion!' says Shakespeare, who knew well what importance to attach to it. (They have been equally obtuse and wrong about him.)

The next thing Colin suggested was a book about historians I have known. In the course of so long a life I have known many of the leading historians in Britain and America. Naturally this means medievalists and modernists, not ancient historians of Greece and Rome. I have known some of them too – notably A.H.M. Jones and Ronald Syme, each of them with a leftist bias. Jones had nothing good to say about Julius Caesar – that can't be right. Syme had nothing good whatever to say about Octavian (later the deified Emperor, Augustus.) That can't be right either – there must have been *something* to say for young Octavian, for him to have won so much support and success, in spite of youth and ill health.

The tutelary deities of this last book I wrote for Colin are G.M. Trevelyan in Britain and Samuel Eliot Morison in the USA. Both were men of genius in my view. Trevelyan, with the usual conventional self-deprecation, would not have this to be; I think that Morison, with his Irish streak to mitigate the Boston purple, would admit the soft impeachment. This was not popular with the inferior. Neither of them, for all their immense achievement, had much of a following, for genius is inimitable. Writers with a thesis to advance, like Frederick Jackson Turner, with his over-popularised Frontier thesis, or irresponsibles with a bias, like A.J.P. Taylor, who thought Hitler not much more to blame for the Second German War than the rest of us – such men make much more noise and are much listened to. Ordinary people are incapable of judging in such matters. Henry James knew: 'Nobody ever understands *anything*.' Franklin Roosevelt, the great Democrat: 'The public never understands.' (He did not say it out loud. The historian, whose duty is to tell the truth, should do so.)

I have done my best to do justice to these eminent historians and interpret their work, a whole bevy of them, perhaps a score. How much I wish Colin were here to see what I have made of them. Naturally, such a book reveals one's own standards, attitudes and prejudices in writing history. People may regard me as a simple follower of Trevelyan, because I agree with him about history as a literary art, an important part of literature, and appreciate the poetry in history. But, intellectually, I share more Namier's tragic view. He had no illusions; neither have I. Trevelyan's early Liberal illusions – about Italy, the Risorgimento and the rest of it – were blasted by the events of our time. Who that is intelligent can have any illusions about the appalling century we have lived through?

Attached as I was to Trevelyan, he never grasped my underlying scepticism and ambivalence, or the combination of the sceptic with the aesthete, as with Burckhardt or Huizinga. So, neither Trevelyan nor Morison, friends as we were, in the simplicity of their hearts, approved of my line about the Puritans, or even appreciated the grounds for it. They were not aesthetes. Kenneth Clark was – he understood the importance of Iconoclasm and perhaps the motives for it. There are plenty of odious people in history, 'fanatics, humbugs and hypocrites' – as Trevor-Roper described my Regicides book (he privately agreed with me). It is the duty of the historian to tell the truth about humans, though they don't like it. Stanley Baldwin's unbeatable humbug was always popular – and see what that led to! I prefer his cousin Kipling's unpopular propensity to face them with the truth.

Nobody noticed the general theme brought home by the book, its main thrust – that humans are made fools of by their beliefs, which are almost always, throughout history, nonsense. One can hardly expect the ordinary ruck to like that either, but the superior minds of Gibbon, Hume and Voltaire understood it very well.

When Colin came to see me on my Cornish headland, perched in bed, we did not have time to discuss all this. With his quick intelligence, and our common Oxford background, I expect that he assumed it already. Also, with his sense of humour, he would recognise how much was to be taken in inverted commas, and how much was dead serious. Ordinary people can't tell, any more than they could with Gibbon or Carlyle or, for that matter, Dr Johnson.

At once we got on, as they say, like a house on fire. There was his readiness for a joke, and we had plenty to laugh about. No need to explain myself with him. There was such a *rapport* that, old as I am – a quarter of a century his senior – I took the liberty of teasing him as an unreconstructed hetero. From time to time, making a point, I flung 'Addison's Walk' at him. He had wondered whether Erasmus and Thomas More had not been sexually attracted to each other! Erasmus was that way, the sainted More decidedly not. Erasmus' fondness was, naturally enough, for the handsome young Mountjoy, his pupil. I had fun teasing a scholar, with his knowledge of the classics, not guessing those familiar facts of life!

I thought of our meeting as preliminary to more, hoping to interest him in my Shakespeare work, which has occupied so much of the later half of my life. Alas, it was not to be, and I was never to know how far it might engage his initiative. The alertness of his mind, the width and speed of engagement with so many interests, the ease with which he dealt with them, were what impressed me, having so little opportunity of knowing him. They, along with humanity and kindness, make his loss, in the prime of his powers, irreparable.

Helen Muir

Around at the Crescent

Colin Haycraft was the first publisher I ever met. 'Dear Mr Haycroft,' I wrote when I sent him my first novel late in 1974, and by that Christmas I had been gathered into an all-consuming new life of wondrous gossip, drink and excitement. It was good luck to have landed by chance with one of the most brainy, colourful figures in a changing publishing scene, who could still recommend all the books on his list. There was also much to be said for being able to deal directly with the chairman in his kitchen where decisions could be made there and then. In years to come, the Duckworth reign of Colin and Anna in Gloucester Crescent will surely still be talked about, as people have gone on talking about the Bloomsbury existence.

It was agreed that Colin would be acting as both publisher and agent for the book and I was invited to my first dinner party, an intimidating gathering of academic authors. An evening of such shocks that I can remember almost every word of it, twenty years later.

Since I was already seeing an old friend that night – a waspish, right-wing civil servant who was fighting alcoholism – I was kindly urged to bring him along with me. When I heard that one of the other guests was a fiery left-wing philosopher, known to have thrown drinks over people's heads if roused, I was even more apprehensive. I told my friend to keep his mouth shut at all costs lest my book be cancelled as a result of some unpleasantness.

He kept it shut to the point of total muteness, although Beryl

Bainbridge battled gamely with him in her compassionate way. His drinkless state of glaring misery cast a gloom over the whole table. When the left-wing philosopher declared that IRA bombing in a Birmingham pub was justified because it led to talks, my friend stood up and left the house.

His departure created such an easing of the atmosphere that I got into what I thought was a genial argument with the red thinker myself. He stood up, saying he could not sit at a dinner table with a person like me, and he also left the house. A second moment of utter horror but, far from allowing it to wreck the dinner, everybody moved chairs like the Mad Hatter's Tea Party; the cigar smoke thickened and the evening gathered momentum.

At one end of the table Colin was loudly insisting that religion and novels were only for women. ('Yes, *yes* ... d'you see?') At the other end, Anna advised awed listeners that a man could breast feed a baby in the jungle if he had to. In the early hours, our welcome well-worn, another philosopher, Brian McGuinness, took me home and we stayed involved for the next fifteen years. As he was godfather to Arthur, and a Duckworth author, and Anna was my editor for three novels, that dinner in Gloucester Crescent was to be the first of many more. Times I treasured as fantastically entertaining and instructive. And forever after, whenever I saw Colin my heart lifted. He was so funny and so fighty and such fun. It is very hard to believe he can be dead.

Home, Colin said, with six children and his office up the road, was like Piccadilly Circus; and images from the 'Duckworth' household in those days keep coming back to me. Sarah, at about two and a half, gently patting the chests of female visitors and hopefully murmuring 'Miluk?'. A self-effacing tutor stepping nervously up the stairs to teach the Haycraft boys. Anna, lurking with Jan beside the Aga, having a fag. Friends streaming through the garden door, past an endless rail of newly washed male shirts, to discuss a project, or seek comfort in a crisis or simply to be there for another raucous debate on the man-woman situation. Colin could spend all night repeating one sentence if it was provocative enough.

I remember him secretly pouring superior drink for the men and unleashing something dreadful on the women. He would give someone the coat off his back, but he wouldn't have parted with any of his finds from the antiquarian book shops. He was a passionate champion of the new books he published himself on the ancient Greeks and as boastful as a little boy about his own bawdy epigrams in Greek.

'I don't approve of it,' Anna said, when the talk became too esoteric. But I think she was as proud of him as he was of her. For many of us they were like two sparring gods – he rational and she religious – who treated everybody as a part of the family.

'Anna never puts a foot wrong.' He was talking of the writing in her letters to him from the house in Wales, before she became Alice Thomas Ellis. As an editor, she not only knew what was wrong, she knew how to put it right. If Colin could have defeated her, I think he would have done; but Anna was outside the rules.

I remember Colin when Joshua was dying and when he was battling to save the firm.

His staff seemed to stay with him for years and years. It was the authors who came and went. Colin had such a marvellous reputation for books but not for business. He was a publisher, he said, not a bank. However, his star author, Beryl Bainbridge, never wavered. He nurtured her when she was starting out, and she remained to give support when she was needed.

The Duckworth magic of Colin's day was very potent. I'm so pleased to have known him. We will all be musing on the memories for the rest of our lives.

One disgruntled author, who felt he'd been done down, had once threatened to 'smash his rotten little face in'.

'I don't think I'll go to Haycraft's funeral,' he said the day before.

They were standing in the aisles in the church. And he was there too.

Derwent May

In Gibbon's Berceau

No one who knew Colin will forget his laughter. It burst out of him in a long, merry, staccato ripple and it had usually been preceded by a display of scathing wit. In his conversation he did not suffer fools gladly, though he was often kindness itself to them in life.

The ignorant and ill-educated regularly received the unsentimental lash of his humour. But Colin could dart his subversive thoughts in any direction. At the Beefsteak Club, of which he was a contented member, the custom is to call all the servants 'Charles'. One day when I was lunching at the long table with him, there were a number of members sitting opposite whose names he did not know. He turned to me, a gleam of pleasure already detectable in his eye, behind the black-framed spectacles. 'Who are all these people?' he said. 'I do wish we could call all the members "Charles"!'.

You might have thought he had no heroes. But he certainly had one, and one who would have appreciated his wit – Edward Gibbon. It cannot be often that publishers give a party for a book they have not published. But on June 27, 1987, Colin celebrated in his Gloucester Crescent garden the completion of Gibbon's *Decline and Fall of the Roman Empire*.

It was exactly two hundred years ago that night that Gibbon finished his great work in his garden in Lausanne. It was 'between the hours of 11 and 12', Gibbon recorded in his *Autobiography*, 'that I wrote the last lines of the last page in a summerhouse in my garden. After laying down my pen, I took several turns in a *berceau,* or covered walk of acacias.'

Thomas Hardy was in that Lausanne garden precisely 110 years later, on June 27, 1897, and wrote a wonderful poem there in praise of Gibbon:

> A spirit seems to pass,
> Formal in pose, but grave withal and grand:
> He contemplates a writing in his hand,
> And far lamps fleck him through the thin acacias.

Hardy even gives this famous critic of Christendom the words of Christ to speak, as though Gibbon was a kind of Saviour of the Age of Reason:

> Anon the leaves are closed,
> With 'It is finished!'

Colin would perhaps not have gone as far as that, but he considered that the *Decline and Fall* and Gibbon's *Autobiography* were 'the two best books in English' – or 'at any rate', he said to me with a sense of more worldly duty, 'the two best books not published by Duckworth'.

The invitation card for the party read '8 p.m. for 11 p.m.'. This mysterious timetable meant that at 11 p.m., after proper and copious libations by all the guests in the garden, Colin mounted the recently-installed iron steps up to the balcony on the front of his house.

It was a warm, still night, much as the night must have been in Lausanne 200 years before. The pergola over Colin's and Anna's garden gate even made me think of Gibbon's *berceau.*

Colin had put on a cut-back frock coat in cream and gold brocade, which Beryl Bainbridge had managed to hire from an East End tailor. Beryl poised herself on the garden wall to take photographs. And there, before assembled friends, Gibbonians and countrymen, Colin read the last paragraph of the mighty history.

I don't see the financial titans of the vast new publishing conglomerates even understanding such a disinterested celebration today.

III

Endings Merry and Sad

Richard Gregory
Andrew Barrow
A.C. Grayling
Tom Haycraft
A.N. Wilson
Melvyn Fairclough
Stoddard Martin

Richard Gregory

Man of all Reasons

The Haycraft family is a cosmological Black Hole. Near approach is dangerous indeed. Irresistibly attracted, one is drawn into a creative world of incredible warmth, beyond any normal laws, with no escape.

An astronomer sucked into a Black Hole would be unable to communicate to anyone outside – for any light, any message – would be trapped within its grip of gravity. Such is the fate of memories of Colin. Trapped in the heads of his friends they are impossible to communicate.

I first met Colin thirty years ago at a restaurant in Soho, where he asked me to write a book for the World University Library. This was a brain-child of George Weidenfeld, midwifed by Colin who put a lot of imaginative thinking into this unusually successful international series of brilliantly illustrated books on all manner of topics. Mine, *Eye and Brain*, was Number One of the series. (Still in print, now by OUP.) This meeting was the first intimation of the Haycraft Black Hole from which there is no escape. Some months before, I had been asked to do just this sort of book by another excellent publisher – Colin won, as usual. The final section was completed in the centre of the Black Hole, in the kitchen of the Gloucester Crescent house where Anna and the Aga ruled supreme.

Disaster struck the Aga (Colin attracted disasters of all kinds). When it emitted hellish smoke and refused to light, I named it the Aga Khan't. This sounded, I hope, better than it looks, somewhat like 'Wagner's music is better than it sounds'.

Colin liked jokes but thoroughly disliked music. He also looked down on fruit. He had many loves: bookshops – whisky – fine claret – winning arguments – parties – Oxford, especially his College, Queen's – being driven long distances, even in a wrong direction. He said that he had only driven once – across Africa – and ever after was entirely unable to control a car.

He could be more than frank on sensitive topics: denigrating most, though not quite all, women and especially – with the marked exceptions of Anna and Beryl Bainbridge – lady novelists. He enjoyed being perverse and was sometimes deliberately unfair; often rude but never crude. When woozy in an illness, he declared that at least he knew from direct experience what it was like to be a woman: 'It is horrible – one can't think, or see anything clearly.'

Although he had been a first-class athlete, and still played real tennis throughout the time I knew him, he disliked fresh air. Or at least, he so preferred reading Latin or Greek in a smoky room that he almost never went out of the Wales house to wander in the meadows or visit the waterfall. He would spend the weekend in an easy chair with whisky and tobacco, deep in a far from easy book in a learned language. Yet he always maintained he preferred the life of a publisher to that of a cloistered scholar, though undoubtedly he could have been a superb professor.[1] I found his knowledge of classics quite intimidating. He found my interest in science unimpressive and rather boring. But he did publish a large volume of my collected papers which could hardly be a commercial success. This was typical of his generosity to his friends.

For Colin, world history and individual development start with classical Greece and should never get far away from their origins in Greek poetry and drama. Philosophy held less interest, except perhaps for Plato, whose prose rather than his ideas attracted Colin. But only his many friends in the classics, for which he did so much to promote, are qualified to comment on this very centre of his intellectual life.

He disliked leaving Gloucester Crescent for even a few hours. When the (old) Old Piano Factory had to be abandoned, it was astonishing how he embraced the (new) Old Piano Factory,

[1] See also pp. 36, 43 and 99. (ed.)

which soon became the centre of his professional life. His enthusiasm remained vivid as ever, though it must have been a blow to leave the quite extraordinary 22-sided building that was his dream incarnate. Within its strange shapes and piles of more or less orderly books, there was continuous activity of persuasion and correction, and occasional parties of unforgettable magnitude and mirth. How could one forget the belly-dancing party, or Mervyn Horder in a bizarre bathing dress, playing the piano?

Evenings with the family were richly rewarding experiences, full of argument and laughter. Watching the children grow was a pleasure for us all. I know Arthur best, indeed seeing him as a nominal god-son. The half-dozen Christmases I shared with them were very special, sometimes in London, sometimes in Wales, and once (rather disastrously through lack of space) in my flat in Bristol. Continually, Anna's involvement with Catholicism contrasted strangely with Colin's doubts on just about everything.

There was a dark side to all this – tragic as the Greek drama he loved. We can never forget the terrible accident to Joshua; the attempts in the hospital over nearly a year to communicate through the mask of no expression to a spirit we felt was still there, hidden within his familiar form. Days before the accident he had been excited by snooker (Colin was thinking of getting a table) and here was Josh snookered beyond escape: impossible ever to forget. (It happened a couple of days after I had done a rather nasty experiment, getting myself anaesthetised very slowly with Ketamine to find the order in which sensations are lost with gradual unconsciousness. That week of Ketamine, a night in the hospital, and a flight to California, was nearly my last.) But perhaps none of us was much more than chorus to Colin's shared dramas.

On the light side, Colin made time to talk and joke, and indeed he was the best companion imaginable. His mind worked so fast and accurately, he could keep umpteen ideas in the air at once and play and juggle with sophisticated concepts or more or less devious plans, which he shared with delight. But books and publishing were never far from his consciousness, the smallest hint of a suggestion evoking a new thought, a new plan. The range of his list was astonishing: as he would say, from philosophy to knitting patterns, with classics and novels and (unfortunately) computer manuals between the extremes. His greatest joy was to capture Oxford dons from OUP, and indeed much of the list of his small independent firm would do credit to a major university press, backed by resources built up over hundreds of years. The achievements of this indomitable individual against the tide of corporations, following the deep irresponsibility of unaccountable accountants – who fail to distinguish between money and wealth – inspired us all and has made him a living legend. There was a wit, a humorous aggressive courage, that made Colin's Duckworth unique among present-day publishers. It was ever intriguing for, as one got to know Colin and his creations, everything became less probable and more interesting. Even his bureau was surprising: it was the desk from which *The Forsyte Saga* had *not* been published, by the old firm of Duckworth before Colin's time. He seemed impetuous, yet his thinking was so wide and deep and logical that he was a man of all reasons.

The last time I saw Colin was typical; but as it was the last time, it is now a precious memory. The evening started with a splendid wine party at Stationers Hall, from where I had arranged to drive to give a talk the next morning in St George's House, Windsor Castle. Of course this didn't work at all as planned. Upon leaving, Colin said, 'Let's have dinner at the Beefsteak'. When I said I had to go to Windsor Castle, he said, 'It's only just round the corner' – and off we went for one of the most delightful evenings I have ever spent – with good conversation, excellent food and claret – above all with my very dear friend Colin. What then? It was late, the M4 was closed, the battery was down on my mobile phone. Everything went wrong, when Colin finally disappeared into the Black Hole.

There is only one thing that makes his going acceptable: the memories he leaves are so strong, one cannot believe that he is not with us still. For Colin burned images in our minds, of his world he shared with us – his and Anna's unique *faction* of fact and fiction and action, that was the irresistible mix of the Haycraft magic.

Andrew Barrow

Merry Clubmen

Colin Haycraft was the cleverest, funniest, friendliest person I have ever met. He had none of the caution, the reserve, the capacity for distance, for blowing hot and cold, the potential prickliness or pomposity which hamper most people in their dealings with others. In fact, I would say our friendship had a doggy quality, a tail-wagging simplicity about it – without anything craven on either side. It was never a meeting of minds or souls. There were no intimate exchanges of private pains or intense discussions about Life, such as I have enjoyed, or suffered, with others. We never discussed our work, our children, or anything like that. Our friendship was, quite simply, friendly.

Yet there were considerable differences between us. Colin was seventeen or eighteen years older than me. He was both a Double First and a brilliant games-player. I am no sportsman and an English 'A' level eluded me even after two attempts. Yet Colin never made me feel inferior. Intelligence, he said flatteringly, was far more important than education. I suppose I was his straight man – perhaps everyone was. I never said anything clever or funny, but he responded to my most solemn offerings with witticisms of his own which made him, then me, roar with laughter. I remember him saying that his mother-in-law's funeral was taking place in Wales. 'Are you sending flowers?' I asked feebly. 'No, I'm sending my wife!' he replied, letting out a hoot of self-congratulatory merriment.

Colin's humour was usually simple. He used simple sentences and short words. He knew the power of schoolboy terms like 'twerp' and 'swot'. He relished minor distinctions such as the difference between 'literary' and 'literate' when applied by a famous hostess we both knew. On learning that the Hawthornden Prize had been won by a writer named Tim Pears, he asked impishly if this was anything to do with the novelist Piers Paul Read.

Colin's laughter, chuckles and laid-back drawl were uplifting and infectious. You felt you were with the most discriminating, most sophisticated man in the world. His arrogance and irreverence, especially to Holy Cows, were wonderfully refreshing. 'Do we need him?' he asked of a widely worshipped, much publicised travel writer. Laughter was perhaps his favourite mode of expression. He laughed often on the telephone and even on one's answering machine – he rang sometimes from his office, full of beans and bursting with unbusinesslike bonhomie.

In person, Colin was small, neat and impressive. His eyes were shrewd, alert and, in spite of what I said earlier, wary. His jaw was firm. He wore cheap but dapper suitings. The bow-tie was a sort of signature or statement – of quite what, I do not know. He carried a brief-case and had the aura of the complete professional, nothing of the fuddy duddy: he looked as you would expect the chairman of an important publishing house to look, yet you knew he took nothing, not even his own job, quite seriously. You sensed he enjoyed his power, just as his staff enjoyed being ruled by him, but underneath his purposeful façade there was a vulnerability, an unprotected quality, which drew you close to him.

I had been vaguely aware of Colin Haycraft's existence for many years. The Old Piano Factory and its legends were on many people's lips. I had even once been taken to dinner at Gloucester Crescent by a friend of Anna's. Colin had sat at the head of the table with no trousers on; but, in spite of this promising beginning, we did not make friends for several years. The breakthrough came in 1992 when Colin published my first novel. *The Tap Dancer* had been rejected by all the big publishers in London and my agent had even proposed 'resting' it for a while. When I suggested trying Duckworth, he said that he loved Colin but was unable to do business with him. Colin's long-established scorn for literary agents was notorious.

In the event, and without much hope of success, I decided to deliver my typescript in person at the Old Piano Factory. To my delight and disbelief, it was accepted for publication a few days later. Colin did the necessary paperwork, but the book's main champion in the firm was Michael Estorick. I remain uncertain to this day as to whether Colin ever read the novel, or even part of it. Anyhow, shortly after the contracts were signed – my advance was a princely £500 – the House of Duckworth plunged into an unseemly boardroom battle and for a while Colin was locked out of his own office. On looking back, I am convinced that these troubles benefited my book. The considerable affection that literary editors had for the firm and its beleaguered chairman guaranteed coverage. *The Tap Dancer* was widely reviewed and even secured two literary prizes. Re-established in his office after buying out one of the major shareholders, Colin seemed thrilled by the book's minor success and during the months that followed we had a series of celebratory lunches together.

It was in the civilised and old-fashioned atmosphere of the Beefsteak Club, where we both happened to be members, that our friendship really took off. I would sometimes arrive at the premises – up a staircase in a corner of Leicester Square – and find my publisher in the cloakroom busily brushing his hair, tufts of which sometimes stuck up like a gamebird's. Then there would be some 'business' at the bar, barks of 'Mr Haycraft? Mr Barrow?' from the steward while we examined the menu and knocked back our first drinks: Colin liked whisky, I needed vodka. Eventually, we would take our place at the long Beefsteak table, where those who knew and loved Colin far outnumbered those he found boring. Colin ate his sausages and mash and other club food like a well-behaved schoolboy. We both drank a lot. Lunch ended with cigars and a pub crawl across Soho – there was no question of a return to the office. One afternoon, after Guinness and brandy at the Coach and Horses, we entered the church in Soho Square. Colin had a fresh cigar in his hand and was rudely shooed away by one of these odd men who hang around in places of worship. The chairman of Duckworth then loudly rebuked this layabout for his lack of Christianity, while suggesting to me that it was his briefcase, not the cigar, which had caused the offence.

On another occasion, I invited him to lunch at my studio in Kensington, along with a highly amusing mutual friend, the cookery writer, Jennifer Paterson. I warned Colin in advance that some builders would also be there, making an extra room in the roof, and might be making quite a din with their drills, etc. Colin declared that these noises would be nothing compared to Jennifer's uproarious merry-making, and this proved to be the case. Our celebrations continued long after the builders had left and only ended when a telephone call came from Colin's secretary to say that he was urgently expected at a meeting with his solicitors.

Business difficulties continued to occupy Colin until the end of his life, but he was never dragged down by them. Some of those who had known him for longer than I considered that these ordeals stripped him of some of his earlier haughtiness, but I saw no sign of this myself. Any anxieties he may have felt were concealed with comic combativeness. One adversary was accused of 'behaving like a woman', though this male chauvinism was surely another comic pose.

There were also meals in the L-shaped kitchen at Gloucester Crescent. 'Now, look,' began one telephone call. 'Anna's gone and bought a chicken ...' An invitation to Sunday lunch followed and a kind of baptism into the closely knit and partly unfathomable world of Colin, Anna and Beryl Bainbridge. This trio were also at the heart, without making their presence felt, of many much larger parties in the same place, highly enjoyable and well-attended events which presented such an attractive and distinguished image of publishing that you forgot about the ugly and boring commercialism of most of the industry. Curiously clinical white bread sandwiches from a table beside the Aga were washed down with a lethally spiked Veuve du Vernay which made you long for more.

Colin was extraordinarily welcoming on these occasions, but I never knew much about him. I knew little of his working methods, his quarrels, his impatience, his reported ruthlessness. Even those who loved him would warn that, in some minor way, he might be taking me for a ride. 'Did *you* get a November statement? *I* didn't,' said Beryl Bainbridge on one occasion; but she and I had already decided that such irritations were a small price to pay for the honour of being published by a man we adored. If Colin was a bit of a rascal, so much the more endearing. I also knew nothing of his scholarship, his skills as a Latin and Greek speaker, his business background. Colin Haycraft – the name seems a crystallisation of his boyishness and cleverness – did not talk about the past, never name-dropped about his former employments or mentioned any of the works he had published. On every occasion that I met him, he concentrated forcefully on the present.

He had an immense appetite for life but a disdain for fashion. He had, I suppose, emerged as a young man in the 1950s and to some extent remained shaped by that decade. Like many of the people I have loved, he was a Londoner. It's difficult to imagine him in any other city, except perhaps Oxford – a world I do not know. He was a reluctant socialite, but a hugely popular and well-established figure on the fringe, or at the very heart, according to one's viewpoint, of London's literary life. He was also well-versed in the life of the streets. He read the *Evening Standard* carefully before lunch. Our West End escapades usually ended with farewells at an Underground station, Colin taking the Northern line, me looking for the Central or the Circle. Sometimes, we would bump into each other again a moment later, an excuse for further merriment before we were both swallowed up into the system.

A.C. Grayling

Heraclitus in Peking

Up the road from the socialist-realist bulk of Peking's Friendship Guesthouse, beyond the cheap concrete austerities of the People's University, near a road junction where – or so it seems – several of Peking's largest open sewers unforgettably meet, stands a market. In the market can be purchased every kind of consumable, including huge bunches of dried tobacco-leaves. When these tobacco-leaves are ignited they emit extremely dangerous narcotic fumes. For this reason they have a particular relation to Colin Haycraft; as follows.

Many years ago one of Colin's authors was living in Peking near the noisome market. He was still a pipe smoker then, and early in his sojourn made persistent near-fatal attempts to inhale the smoke of the Chinese tobacco. The consequences – the sensations, the spasms, the wretchednesses of that Duckworth author after each attempt, only marginally less horrible to him than giving up smoking altogether – defy retelling. It would take a Sterne to describe them, as he described Uncle Toby's sensations upon inadvertently dropping that piping-hot chestnut into his trousers. And then suddenly Colin began sending his author, unasked – as if he had read his mind across six thousand miles – a regular supply of Three Nuns Best.

We know people by their fruits; and this was a peach. Kindness is not, thank heaven, rare in this world, but it is infrequent enough. Only consider the author's plight: tobacco-less in a far country, unable (so he then believed; and belief makes the fact) to think unless smoking; obliged therefore to inhale raw Chinese fumes – and then to get a parcel of excellent blend every month, like clockwork! Author and publisher were already friends, but those circular tobacco tins were as Polonius' hoops of steel.

That smoker and this essayist are one. I was spending a year as a visiting lecturer in Peking, where Bertrand Russell – far more famously, and sixty years before – had done the same. The proofs of a book were passing between Colin at the Old Piano Factory and me at the Youyi Bingguan that year, taking longer on each leg as increasingly puzzled security officials scrutinised the hilarious scrawled messages and Latin couplets, most of them obscene, sent by Colin in each parcel. Somewhere in the Forbidden City there now lies a Haycraft archive, barred to all but men of mature years and grave disposition.

Colin was much in Peking that year. He was there in his letters, dibbling-duck postcards, and (not least) parcels of tobacco tins; there, in other words, in personality rather than in person, for like the Venerable Bede he was no traveller in the physical sense. He winged whole heavens when among his books; approaching the gate of 22 Gloucester Crescent one could see him journeying thus, sitting in a low chair in his study above the scullery – a little room of exactly the kind Leigh Hunt described as perfect for reading, with its tall window overlooking the Crescent's trees. But to get Colin on a Peking-bound aeroplane would have taken more miracles than all the calendar's saints could muster. He once made plans to accompany me to Norfolk for a weekend; we never of course actually went; but it shows he did not think that, beyond a four-mile radius of Charing Cross (and excepting Oxford, of which, speaking geographically, he anyway thought Camden was an extension), the rest of the world consisted of Ancient Rome in one direction, and the Eighteenth Century in the other. There was Wales too, of course; but that, with its unexplained laughter, belongs chiefly to Anna.

One of J.I.M. Stewart's *Patullo* characters says of another, 'He was far too gifted to be a don'.[1] That is exactly true of Colin, who was a Double First and a Blue in the widest possible senses. He was supremely gifted in the arts of conversation and friendship. Some allege that he could be beastly (and indeed I once heard

---

[1] See also pp. 36, 43 and 90. (ed.)

him saying marvellously rude things into a telephone receiver), but to friends he was always – absolutely always – welcoming, cheerful, brimming with enjoyment. Even in difficult times he chuckled and joked; even when ill he made light, hating to speak of doctors and their pills. He preferred always to talk of matters classical, historical, philosophical, bibliographical, linguistical – and of course anything that smacked of gossip, which he loved. He also loved making trouble: at dinner parties he would issue wildly provocative remarks and enjoy the resulting fracas, safe behind his bow-tie and irresistible grin.

I only once saw Colin at loss for a remark. We were among the guests of a restaurateur in his Shaftesbury Avenue premises. He had invited us – Colin and Anna, myself and partner – as representatives, in our different capacities, of the louche world of letters, to mingle with a distinguished collection of society folk, including a superannuated ex-Cabinet Minister and a grossly rich young Duchess. When the gentlemen changed places before pudding, Colin and I found ourselves flanking the latter. My attempts to converse foundered on her puzzlement at my suggestion – she having a numerous staff of nannies and maids – that bringing up two infants might be tiring. So she turned to Colin and this conversation (I report it verbatim) ensued:

Duchess: 'What do you do?'

Colin: 'I'm a publisher.'

Duchess: 'Oh – books?'

Colin: 'Yes.'

Duchess: (after a short meditative pause) 'I read one once.'

Colin: (in some shock) 'Which one?'

Duchess: 'I can't remember – I think it was *Watership Down*.'

Colin: uncharacteristic silence.

Duchess: (after another meditative pause) 'But I don't think I finished it.'

Colin needed a Boswell. He talked so well and funnily that one felt the usual mistaken desire that he would do as the angel required of Tobit, and write it down in a book. Good talkers do not always make good authors, but Colin would have done so; he was a scrupulous lover of English, and wrote beautifully. But without his intonation and sparkle some of his utterances might invite misunderstanding – especially in respect of his feminist

credentials. He liked to say that women should restrict themselves to fiction, and men to non-fiction, and that he would never
accept a book of either genre from the unsuitable sex. Of course,
he did; for he was only *half* joking. He also thought religion was
exclusively for women, which was one reason why he was wont
to say, in reference to the large number of offspring he had, that
he was not a Catholic in theory, only in practice. (I once heard
someone ask him if he was a Catholic. He replied, 'Certainly not!
I'm a gentleman.')

Christmas parties at the Old Piano Factory make one focus for
shared memories of Colin when friends speak of him. We were
invited to them by Anna and the Directors, never by Colin
himself. They were apt to be rich in incident, as when Freddie
Ayer, attending his last Duckworth party and too ill to climb the
famous iron spiral staircase, had to be winched up by Colin in
the book hoist. But Colin's most memorable party was his bicen-
tennial celebration of the completion of *Decline and Fall* with
Colin himself appearing on his balcony in eighteenth-century
garb to read Gibbon's description of that immortal night in
Lausanne:

It was on the day, or rather, night, of the 27th June 1787,
between the hours of eleven and twelve, that I wrote the
last lines of the last page in a summerhouse in my garden.
After laying down my pen I took several turns in a *berceau*,
or covered walk of acacias, which commands a prospect of
the country, the lake and the mountains. The air was
temperate, the sky was serene, the silver orb of the moon
was reflected from the waters, and all nature was silent. I
will not dissemble the first emotions of joy on the recovery
of my freedom, and perhaps the establishment of my fame.
But my pride was soon humbled, and a sober melancholy
was spread over my mind, by the idea that I had taken
everlasting leave of an old and agreeable companion, and
that whatsoever the future fate of my *History*, the life of the
historian must be short and precarious.

The first time Colin came to dinner at my home he brought
with him a very large bottle of Scotch, prepared for the worst in

the household of a teetotaller. Finding a plentiful supply of booze, he took the bottle home unopened. On subsequent visits he even brought his cigars, although latterly forbidden them. He was quite properly mistrustful of teetotal, ex-smoker vegetarians, but he was a forgiving and tolerant friend, and although it pained him to see how much water and spinach I consumed, he was always mild in his complaints about it.

Colin on social occasions was a fountain of witticisms and (as everyone got drunker) outrageous remarks. But still better were tête-à-tête conversations with him in his smoky Old Piano Factory office, or over extremely long lunches in Charlotte Street, or during late-night drives back from Oxford dinners. His large stock of reading and intelligence was always ready, a quick and open archive. He was inquisitive, enquiring, sharply alert to what was happening in most of the academic fields he published. Although he professed dilettantism, he was a profounder scholar than many knew. One laughed much and learned much, in those happy hours of talk with him.

A mutual friend (the editor of this volume) and I lately disagreed over some of Colin's tastes, he saying that Colin liked best to read Greek, I that he preferred the Latin authors. Memory plays one false: when Colin talked to me of the classics, most mentioned were Virgil and Horace (and Tacitus), but I might wrongly have inferred therefore that his preference lay with them. It now seems extraordinary to be uncertain about so germane a matter with such a friend; but Colin's topics of conversation were vastly diverse: everything captured him, and seemed a favourite.

Colin was sometimes dilatory in paying his authors their royalties. (A month before he died he sent me a large cheque for *years'* worth of back-royalties from several books. Like the tobacco, it was unasked and unexpected: sadly prescient, a settling of accounts.) This was because Duckworth's survival mattered above most things, and because if some authors had been paid others would not have been published. Colin simply got on with the job of surviving and publishing, and in general he published books he liked, or by people he liked, and it was relatively late in the day that the harsher commercial exigencies forced themselves. Some of the books Colin published will live, though they might never sell in large numbers. Books that will live! – *that* is really something.

What passes between friends is too much their own, and too much in quantity, to bear recording. When news came of Colin's death the poignant lines by William Cory sprang immediately to mind – I am sure they occurred also to many others, because the verse is peculiarly apt in Colin's case – and they sum all up for me, because this is how it feels:

> They told me, Heraclitus, they told me you were dead,
> They brought me bitter news to hear and bitter tears to
>   shed.
> I wept as I remember'd how often you and I
> Had tired the sun with talking and sent him down the sky.
>
> And now that thou art lying, my dear old Carian guest,
> A handful of grey ashes, long, long ago at rest,
> Still are thy pleasant voices, thy nightingales, awake;
> For Death, he taketh all away, but them he cannot take.

Tom Haycraft

Beyond the Beaver Lodge

I *think* my father taught me how to play chess. Leastways I do know how to play, though somewhat indifferently, and have, if not exactly a solid memory of it, a feeling that he and I once shuffled chess pieces across a board.

I *know* he taught me the Greek alphabet. Instead of nursery rhymes I'd recite *Alpha, Beta, Gamma, Delta* while seated on his knee. It was only much later that I learnt the English alphabet. I still remember the Greek, though I've always had a mental block after *Tau*. I think forgetting the last five letters was my earliest attempt at rebellion.

To my father Greek held a wealth of enjoyment and, having been brought up on the classics, as far as he was concerned that was the only proper education. When we (his children) were young, he did his best to try to instil some of his passion into us and a stream of Latin tutors were engaged to try and deposit some knowledge into our apathetic minds. I'm not sure if my brothers retained any of their classical education, but I can still conjugate *amo*.

Another memory from my youth was being bribed to go with him to second-hand bookshops when he was building his library. The bribe was usually one of those awful Wall's ice creams that seemed to be all you could get in the '60s. The form they took was of a small yellow brick wrapped in paper. They invariably had a tacky scum adhering to them, and were eaten between two cardboard-like wafers. I always felt it a raw deal having to spend most of a perfectly good Saturday in a dusty, dark antiquarian

book shop with never a comic in sight and a Wall's sausage
by-product as compensation.

I know better now. An Oxford bookshop recently sent someone
round to look at my father's classical library, and he declared it
one of the six best working collections in private hands in the
country. Dad would have laughed and said 'what on Earth do you
mean, *one* of the six best ...'

When we were small my mother rented a house in the wilds
of North Wales to which we would all de-camp during school
holidays. That is all of us except Dad, who would remain
blissfully alone in London existing on a diet of Greek bread,
cheese, broad beans and *Retsina*. He only very occasionally
ventured to Stacros, as the cottage was named, as he was
unable to see the point of the countryside. He would arrive
with friends, wine and whisky, not forgetting a few volumes of
Horace to give him something to *do* during the day. It was
always something of an adventure when he arrived and the
pace at our small cottage would change drastically for the
short time he'd be there. We never had electricity at Stacros
and used candles in the evenings, which generally meant we
all went to bed early. However we did have a supply of ancient
Tilley lamps that my mother was deadly scared of, but which
my father would haul out as soon as he arrived. Mum was full
of dire warnings about excess of pressure, explosions, fire and
so on and banned us children from going anywhere near them.
It was always with grim excitement and expectation of calamity
that we'd watch Dad pump up the pressure.

On the day he was due to arrive we children would rise early
and set out to stand vigil on the rough forestry track that he
would pass along. Having hours to while away before his
arrival we'd cast about for something to do. This usually
meant setting up a road-block of logs hauled out of the forestry
and then stationing ourselves in ambush among the trees with
supplies of fir cones ready to pelt all who should pass. Generally no one would and we'd drift off disconsolately back to the
house for Spam sandwiches, leaving the roadblock in place,
being too feckless to take it down. When Dad finally arrived it
was always with a driver mystified by the beaver lodge-like

pile of logs that would have to be cleared before they could continue.

My father stopped driving a car in 1959. After leaving Oxford he drove all over America (with the handbrake on) and then went to work in Nigeria as a correspondent for the *Daily Mirror*, and drove all round that country. He told me that this was no mean feat as the Nigerian roadbuilders had failed to grasp fully the intricacies of their task, and had cambered their roads into the middle. When he finished his stint in Africa and came back to London, his international driving licence expired, necessitating the acquisition of a British one so he could continue driving the Austin 7 he had purchased for ten pounds. His examiner, he fondly remembered, failed him for a great number of infractions including *steering*.

He never bothered to take another test, as by this time my mother had two children and was expecting her third and he didn't fancy the years of family chauffeuring he would inevitably have had to do. Anyway the door had fallen off the car.

It seemed to me that my father was happiest when having huge parties at the Old Piano Factory. There were many over the years, usually held to launch a book he was publishing. I remember one to introduce a book about belly dancing, written by a rather suburban English lady. After the guests had imbibed copious draughts of 'Colin's Killers' (a concoction made from fizzy white wine, cointreau, a sugar cube and maraschino cherry) the 'entertainment' began. A stage had been erected in the middle of the circular piano factory, rather like a boxing ring in appearance. The authoress, clad in veils and sequins and clutching castanets, proceeded to entertain the company with her craft, backed by a cheap tape player emitting a middle-eastern caterwaul. At some point in the proceedings a rival group of belly dancers gate-crashed the party and, uninvited, climbed aboard the stage. Our authoress fled, weeping, into my father's arms. Most of the guests were unaware of what was happening, and the evening degenerated from then on, with usually well-behaved literary types taking off their shirts in order to gyrate their flabby bellies on stage.

I remember thinking at the Requiem Mass we held for my father in St Etheldreda's how much he would have enjoyed the party we had afterwards in the crypt. It was just like one of those wonderful Duckworth parties of old, albeit without belly dancers. In retrospect I wish someone had thought to serve 'Colin's Killers'.

He's missed.

A.N. Wilson

A Rather Serious Person

Colin Haycraft's habitual strong talk, delivered in a drawl, and invariably followed by gales of laughter, is something which I miss intensely – but to write it down would be to run the danger of making it seem boorish or unkind which, mysteriously, it never was. 'Religion is really for women and queers.' 'One can't forgive Hitler for ruining so many good ideas.' 'Only women should write novels – fiction is a branch of gynaecology.' (If, in riposte, one mentioned Balzac, Tolstoy or Dickens, the laughter merely increased, and when it died down, he would add, 'Quite.') 'Why do geographers talk about the Indian sub-continent? You either have a continent or you don't. There's no such thing as a sub-continent. On the other hand, sub-incontinent is not a bad concept. X. does not actually wet himself, but when he has been to lunch I put his chair in the garden for an airing.' 'It's embarrassing when one's wife writes novels, but at least Anna's novels are *good* novels. Imagine being Y [a friend married to a universally esteemed novelist]. One would never live it down.'

This last remark was his way of saying that he was immensely proud of Anna's work; just as he was proud of publishing the novels of Beryl Bainbridge. 'Beryl's books are so good, they might have been written by a man.' (Never mind that only women and queers bother to write novels; all that mattered in such throwaway talk was that one should not come too close to seriousness. And that, paradoxically, was because Colin was rather a serious person.)

He could have echoed those lines of MacNiece:

But in case you should think my education was wasted
    I hasten to explain
That having been to the University of Oxford
    You can never really again
Believe anything that anyone says and that of course is an
    asset
    In a world like ours ...

He loved Oxford (and in a slightly different way, Wellington)
with a passion, and it was sometimes difficult, during our talks
in some Camden Town restaurant ('We could go in here, though
I always think that Greek food is a contradiction in terms') to
remember that we were not in a Common Room or Hall. His talk
was what non-academic guests in Oxford always hope they will
get at High Table and so seldom do.

His school and university obsessions extended well beyond his
own life or friends. 'Cardinal Manning had a bad start in life.
Harrow and Balliol.' Near apoplectic laughter. 'A deadly mixture. You couldn't expect anything better from him after that.'
He liked to imagine which schools or colleges might have been
suitable for figures of antiquity. I remember he thought it possible that Jesus had been to Eton, but St Paul was definitely a
Wykehamist. Seneca went to Uppingham, then Balliol.

His vision of things was shaped by Gibbon, whom he read
constantly. He did not usually read him in order, but after his
first serious illness, a year or so before he died, he started again
at the beginning and read *The Decline and Fall* through. He
liked to say that it was the best book in the English language and
the second best book was Gibbon's *Autobiography*. Next to these,
he loved Syme's *The Roman Revolution* (he gave me my copy,
inscribed, 'the best book of history since E. Gibbon's') and
Boswell. The character of Johnson was something to which he
frequently referred in his oblique chat, opining that Gibbon and
Johnson had compatible views about everything except religion,
which – for Colin – was a demonstration of the fact that the
religious viewpoint was largely determined by temperament.
Johnson's fear of hell was an extension of his melancholy-
madness.

Like his hero Gibbon, Colin bestrode two eras, holding up the values of the modern world and the Christian dispensation to a constant comparison with those of the ancients – and hence, to derision. He liked to address his mind to such questions as whether Cicero would have enjoyed possessing a telephone, or what was the Greek for 'Enjoy!' (as said by American waiters). He decided it was χαῖρε!

His passion for publishing, his preparedness to risk all his worldly wealth, all his peace of mind, and in the end, his health in order to keep Duckworth afloat was really guided by his heroic desire to keep classics and philosophy alive. The list of works which he published (many of which he commissioned and inspired) is a tribute to his range and his enthusiasm and learning. But he would not have been happy publishing the same titles as the employee of some University Press. Not only was he bullishly (it could be said fatally) addicted to being his own boss, but he liked the eclectic nature of what Duckworth was able to produce as a small independent house. Who else – to choose a random sample of books which Colin published in the last couple of years of his life – would have included, on the same list as his serious classical stuff, the autobiography of John Major's brother, Terry Major-Ball, or a re-issue of Marion Crawford's *The Little Princesses*?

Like other publishers I have known, he had a short attention-span when his own wares were in question. Very excited for a fortnight or so about a particular book he had brought out, he would quickly lose interest in it and wish to be on to the next project. Contrary to what his fellow-publishers believed, some Duckworth books did actually sell quite well; but this did not seem to interest Colin very much, even in the days of his deepest financial anxiety. I remember asking him how one particular book had 'done'. It had received extravagant praise from reviewers and my office at the *Evening Standard* (where I work as Literary Editor) received innumerable telephone calls from readers who had been into book shops, only to be told that the book had sold out.

'Surely you are going to do a reprint?' I asked Colin.

'I don't think X' – the author – 'needs the money' was the reply.

'But what's that got to do with it – you never pay your authors anyway?'

'I know I don't. It's the first rule of publishing.'

He regarded those publishers who paid large amounts of money in advance to their authors as fools, and he watched with detached contempt as, one after the other, they were all taken over by 'conglomerates'.

His determination that this would never happen to Duckworth in his lifetime led to some extraordinary cliff-hangers, some soul-destroying legal battles, and the destruction of all repose. 'I used to lie in my bath and recite the Odes of Horace, or just let my thoughts wander. Now I think about lawyer's letters all the time.'

I have not perhaps made Colin sound a very nice man, or a man, in Mr Major's famous phrase, 'at ease with himself'. Perhaps in the strict sense of the words, he was not. But he had the old-fashioned gift of friendship, extended over a wide range to people of both sexes, and to many different types, classes and age-groups. He was attentive, as Johnson said a man should be, to keeping his friendships 'in good repair'. A lunch, or a telephone-conversation during which some scholarly question, or some half-finished piece of gossip had cropped up, would always be followed with a post-card, usually posted through the door by hand, settling the point at issue, and suggesting another meeting soon.

The last such came through the door a few days before he died. It was stuck into Robert Garland's *Religion and the Greeks*, which he had just published. 'Here is more grist to your mill', it read. 'The preface alone is enough to show what sensible attitudes there were before the invention of Christianity.'

My next appointment with Colin was to attend his funeral. The congregation was vast – as big as any I ever saw at a private obsequy. That would have pleased him; and if some of the Roman Catholic prayers would have caused him to raise an eyebrow and look quizzically over his spectacles, they would not have surprised him *much*. He was a Gibbonian, not an atheist. 'Freddie (Ayer) goes too far. If you say you're an atheist it implies you take religion *seriously*, for Christ's sake.'

Melvyn Fairclough

The Common Touch

I didn't know Colin that well because I met him only a short while ago, in 1990. It was in his Dickensian office at the Old Piano Factory in Camden, a short walk up the road from his home. The round central work-room, shaped like a brick tent with a short, wide, cone-shaped roof, piled high with books and boxes, where people worked away at word processors, was solidly Victorian. Like Colin it had lots of character and charm.

He flipped through the manuscript of my book about Jack the Ripper and asked quite a few relevant questions. He agreed with me that the book should appeal not only to the morbidly curious, but also to highbrows and the vast army of 'Ripperologists', and that it should not be found fault with by historians. Happily our opinions were in agreement on many subjects, despite our different backgrounds. It was always a pleasure to talk with him, and it was a surprise to discover that his opinions, although those of a classical scholar who always wore a bow-tie, were not at all stuffy, as I had half-expected them to be. Among those I count as friends he was the best educated, yet he was never too clever, and far too kind and well mannered to make me feel inadequate. But though he was attentive and charming most of the time, he could be abrasive to those he considered fools. Also, like Johnson whom he liked to quote, he hated cant. He mistrusted 'worthies', preferring to trust honest hypocrites whom he considered more human and humane.

My own education was basic and I left school at sixteen to go to art college, but because of some misunderstanding I had to leave because I could not get a grant. Nevertheless Colin was aware that I had tried to educate myself as best I could. (I was pleased as Punch when he read something in my manuscript which he thought was historically inaccurate and found, upon checking, that it was right after all.) The point I am clumsily trying to make is that Colin was never condescending, very generous spirited, most encouraging and made me feel his equal. Sometimes he laughed at my jokes almost as loudly as he laughed at his own, which he did often and infectiously.

After Colin edited my manuscript more information became available which had to be included, and he edited it again. I seem to remember this happened four times, resulting in a finished product far better than I could have produced unaided. By seeing what he did I learned a lot.

It was through Colin that I met a wide range of people I would not otherwise have met, because he always asked me to his parties. I particularly remember a luncheon at his house where there were several women journalists. I think two were from the *Daily Telegraph*. As was often the case, Colin behaved a little mischievously and deliberately made several outrageously sexist remarks. Of course the women, whom Colin had not met before, swallowed the bait, and he proceeded to reel them in, only to throw them back into the turbulent water and start again. He tickled them as one tickles a trout, and before they left they were caught. He had them laughing at him and with him, and at themselves, and brought about their temporary conversion to his views through his immense charm and incisive wit. It was always thus. People delighted in his political incorrectness which was rarely unkind to individuals and, more often than not, spot-on.

Colin had surprisingly simple tastes for one used to dining in hall at his beloved Oxford, or at his clubs, the Beefsteak or the Jesters. More than once, while I was restoring some furniture at his house, I saw him lunch on a little bread and butter and a glass of wine, or perhaps just a tomato and some bread with a sprinkling of olive oil. I suppose that he acquired this taste in Italy where he spent some early childhood years with his mother, after his father was murdered in India. A couple of times I had supper with him and Beryl Bainbridge in a greasy-spoon.

They both had sausage, egg and chips which, by their own account, was one of their favourite meals. One evening recently Beryl dined with me and a mutual friend in a trendy Camden Town restaurant. We ordered something French while Beryl ordered the breakfast: sausage, egg and chips.

On one occasion when I was with Colin in his office, surrounded by books and framed jackets published by Duckworth in the twenties and thirties, he had a telephone call from a fellow classicist. Colin wrote something down in ancient Greek and laughed loudly. Afterwards he tried to explain to me, in vain as it turned out, the play on words which he found immensely funny. Latin and ancient Greek, two dead languages, were, to him, very much alive and kicking. Often late at night he could be found sitting downstairs in his dining room with a glass of wine at his side, a small cigar in his hand and a lamp shining over his shoulder to illuminate his treasured Homer, Horace or Virgil, or whatever he was reading.

Colin was someone I could telephone at his home or office, day or evening, to ask advice, or perhaps to translate a Latin tag or motto. He was always helpful without making me feel he couldn't spare the time. If he didn't have a ready answer he knew where to find it, and finding would be 'no trouble at all'.

I grew very fond of him and was flattered when his wife Anna said that he was fond of me.

He was a most uncommon man, yet had the common touch. I wish I'd known him longer.

Stoddard Martin

The Last Act of His Passing

We joked about whether the pathetic fallacy would attend at the last act of Colin's passing. In the event, we set out for the burial armed with umbrellas. Spits of rain in the driveway gave way to flashes of sun on the road. The Welsh hills lit up yellow, green as paint, then fell back into shadow as clouds re-obscured swaths of blue in the sky.

What would have been appropriate? Rain? Heaven's tears? There was plenty of water pent up in the eye. Alone of the group, I had brought my dark glasses. Colin's sons had left theirs in London, though they had worn them to the funeral three days before. Perhaps no one expected the sun in North Wales. Anyway, now that the mourners were down to an inner core, what did it matter who showed his grief?

On the other hand, why not be stoical? This was not Russia, or America. Colin himself represented the stiff upper lip: a last generation of True Brit brought up in the war on tins of baked beans and in chilly boarding schools. Yet I remembered the last time he had passed through this churchyard, just two years before, for the marriage of his third son, Thomas. While that replica of himself stood at altar with bride, I had seen Colin glance at his wife with water fogging the lenses of his glasses. It had seemed most unlike him. But how much more interesting is the soul of a man who only dares to show it ever so rarely?

No one gave instructions. As the hearse made its way through the hedgerows, we fell in behind in order of rank. At the front

walked Anna, looking every bit her parts as widow and matri-
arch of tribe. Beside her was Sarah, once a annoying pre-teen but
now at 23 so stunning and sweet as to evoke quite different
sensations. Then came the four sons, each etched and differenti-
ated in adulthood, all the more so as they rose to the occasion of
father's death: William, 37, precisely Colin in build, yet entirely
himself in candour and humility; Thomas, 34, whose jokes preserved in their style a side of Dad imperishable to all who had
known him; Oliver, 32, without sideburns and quiff of his years
as a rock-star, reborn now as another replica of *pater*, even down
to the pin-striped suit; at last, slim Arthur, 28, though in some
ways, as William remarked, the eldest and most 'sterling' of the
lot.

Others followed, heads down or eyes to the sky, chatting
desultorily with those walking beside: John Haycraft and wife,
themselves dealing with the aftermath of a sequence of strokes
like the ones which presaged Colin's end; Ray Davies and Deborah Blake, his colleagues in Duckworth, who had known every
interval of his working life for a decade or more; Richard Gregory, craggy, fleece-haired, an eminent scientist of the mind who
for years had been in thrall to the fruits of Colin's brain, his
cartoon-like distortions of himself and others by which one
passed a hilarious half-hour; a handful of neighbours and friends
until, last but not least, one of the enduring delights of his life,
Beryl Bainbridge, backbone of Duckworth's list and balancer of
its books with her novels, sprightly and beloved with her kind,
dancing soul, which would miss his as much as any.

Beryl snapped photos from the edge of the procession. At last,
we reached the shady churchyard. Silence. A wet breeze passed.
The boys concentrated on their duty of easing the coffin out of
the hearse. How far he had travelled! How much he must have
longed to reach the spot next to his second son, Joshua, where he
could take his final rest.

Final rest? What clichés! How he would have risen up in scorn
at the phrase! How little time he had for discussion of such topics
as what might happen after *his* death. He might listen sympa-
thically about someone else's mortality, but when it came to his
own we got short shrift. A man in a hurry has little time for such

things. Wet and effeminate. On to the next subject, introduced by some Latin joke.

He was not made for this, but for life – so we must all have been thinking as we gathered by the grave. The boys slid the coffin onto the spars over the hole. Much more silence. They stepped back beside mother and sister. We gazed.

At last the priest spoke.

Priest?! 'Religion is for women and queers!' – We had heard him uproarious on the subject for years, even in front of his wife and a gay friend, both of whom were Catholic converts. 'I'll get you in the end, darling!' Anna would retort, never one to be bested by his pagan sallies. And he would laugh. We all would. He knew his role in the playlet, she hers. They acted out an ancient dialectic between classical zest for Life-*qua*-Life and Christian endurance through this Vale of Tears. Together, it was terrific: it seemed a whole truth. Together they had been conflict and resolution: the great opposites in struggle which, by some Goethean synthesis, produced a *tertium quid*: more intense, on a higher plane.

The priest spoke: a kind little man with a lonely parish of less than two hundred souls, stretched across the dark hills from the coast down to Welshpool. Later he would ask if he had been too brief. It was just right, we assured him. There had been a full Requiem already in London, with three hundred people spilling out of the rear of the church. Some had feared then that Colin was squirming in his coffin, especially when the holy water and incense were shaken about. But here at the graveside few words were needed. The old service, which Anna favoured – that was enough.

'Get on with it!' we might have heard him whisper. Then silence. The wet, gentle breeze.

Anna stepped forward, very handsome in black. She threw a handful of dirt down the hole. Down, down, down, onto his blond-wooden bier, over which her beloved body would rest in some future year, beside the dead son and waiting for the others, who in time would populate the little Welsh churchyard to such an extent that a passer-by might imagine that the whole valley had once been a Haycraft ancestral domain.

She stepped back. Through the film on our eyes, we saw Arthur come forward. A clod of dirt sounded. Then Thomas and William and Ollie and Sarah and then – there was nothing.

'Where there is nothing/There is God,' Yeats wrote.

Celtically, the breeze passed. A wan sun scattered light across the ewe-trees. We stood, chilled and dazed. John Haycraft stared, a shade of horror on his face. We all tried not to think about what he must have been thinking.

'Don't worry, brother,' a voice seemed to say. 'It all comes soon enough.'

Across the headstones, Beryl whispered: 'Isn't death weird? I can't imagine what it's like to be down there.'

'I've never thought about my own death once through this,' I murmured.

'Ah, darling, that's because you're young.'

Perhaps. At any rate, I was not Elizabethan enough in that moment to envision a slow feast by worms.

Eventually, we made our way back, singly, doubly, no longer in procession, each in his private thoughts. It was true I had not wondered about my own death, or even my health, in the nine days since Colin's last stroke. This was remarkable when you consider how wet we Americans can be about a twinge in an arm or ache over an ear. My parents died of strokes. Colin had two before the one that took him off, one shockingly in my presence. I had spent the following year feeling small, hysterical symptoms. ('A man can't be hysterical,' he would object. 'The word comes from ὑστέρα, which means womb.') Now, at least temporarily, my neuroses were swept off by his real agony. It was one of many unexpected ways in which he had been a kind of Christ.

'A kind of Christ?! What preposterous nonsense!'

But was it? Why had so many loved him? Why had they spilled out of the medieval church for his Mass? It was true that a Duckworth party had been scheduled for the crypt afterwards, but no one this time had just shown up for free drinks. The silence with which the service had ended intimated deep, pervasive shock. A flash of Colin had risen when Thomas had read the lesson, dead-pan, sceptical, unreligious. Another glimpse had passed when Richard Gregory, in the funeral oration, had evoked him sitting by the fire in Wales reading Horace, oblivious to the Celtic beauty outside. That Welsh thing was Anna's — un-English, aesthetic. 'You go to Wales, darling: I'll have a whale of a time here!' And so he would.

We had missed him in the church. When the coffin had passed, silence waited for his last laugh and merry riposte. None came, to our shock.

It was hard to believe.

What had passed? An Englishman born to a family of place and privilege, still in the age of the Raj; an Englishman brought up to despise the effeminate concerns of the body, unlike us ortho-donted, over-analysed Americans; an Englishman expected to be hale and alert, from prep school through public school to university. Having not known his father, he had had to create his own identity, out of the example of masters, machismo of fellow schoolboys, grit of the essential self. His mother had been 'mad' in the inspired way of English eccentrics: mad for the scandalous vignette from history or her times; equally at home in gossip of the Directoire, the court of Lola Montez, or the pin-up of British manhood in Colin's youth, Winston Churchill.

He amazed his contemporaries for academic and athletic excellence. How could it have been otherwise? What alternative had he for getting love, giving pleasure, than climbing an establishment pole? Clever, energetic, he went to work for a cousin, Cecil King, proprietor of the *Mirror* and one of the odder manifestations of English machismo in the post-Churchill age. Colin observed; he absorbed; he moved on. He lived on personality — something quite different from the legendary British charm. Strutting like a jovial bantam-cock, he never lounged in the manner of Eden-era Etonians. His ideal of manhood was active, roguish, more democratic at base, though never quite political. He had little in common with long-legged scions of an Edwardian high-tide; though he professed to despise him, he developed more in the shape and manner of their admirer and parodist, Waugh.

Barking, scarifying the world with 'incorrect' remarks, he made himself seem a last bastion of values of the much-despised White European Male, Anglo-Saxon style. Never bitchy in the post-Waughian manner of homosexual chic, he did not plump himself up through upper-class connections or a *Brideshead Revisited* snobbery of Faith. Snobbery was not his vice. Excellence was. Prose like Gibbon's; thought like Dr Johnson's. Colin was prejudiced. Unshakably, he believed that the English eighteenth century had been a pinnacle of civilisation: that good sense and *bon tempérament* had won out then over the romantic excesses of the Elizabethans ('Shakespeare, what? can't understand him'), decadence of the Jacobeans, severity of the Commonwealth, triviality of the Restoration and effeminate passions ('a man can't be passionate, only women can') of the Byron era which followed. Like Churchill, he believed that the great age of his people had been announced by the victories of Marlborough, reasserted by those of Wellington and brought to its climax by the 'finest hour' of Churchill himself.

His passing, then, might have been of a type of 'last Englishman'. Perhaps no one else was thinking this as we regrouped in a great, grey-stoned Welsh barn. No doubt I was not thinking so expansively then either. In fact, I was speaking with a Welsh media person about Neil Kinnock, Tony Blair and the future of the Labour Party. Colin would have been impatient. In his heart, he was Tory. All his kind were, despite the flutterings of Cecil King around the Labour right, until that bizarre moment when he allegedly tried to despose Wilson and replace him with a directorate led by Mountbatten. This was part of what was passing: the patriotic fantasies of an essentially non-political class. This is part of what Colin had been: an anti-political, once-Labourite, instinctive Tory, living bon-vivantishly in a generation which fiddled while London burned. His favourite book had been *The Decline and Fall of the Roman Empire*. The context of his life had been the slide and collapse of a British one.

And so to the stories of his shallowness and vices: his sad dealings with money; his jocular disparagements of Americans, Jews, old Etonians, anyone likely to be able to get on top of him; his tendency to wriggle, expressed by one put-upon backer, 'The problem with Colin is that every time he comes up with someone to save him, he starts looking for someone to save him from his saviour.' A story of Britain in her decline: first a special relationship with the Americans, then when they get too big to take

Colin and Anna with (*from left*) Arthur, William and Sarah

Colin at Menton, aged 6

Colin, aged 9, with his mother and brother John in Brittany

Colin at Eastbourne, aged 10

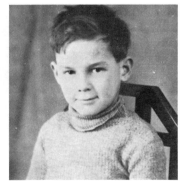

Colin at Queen's College, Oxford

Colin playing squash

Colin in the USA in 1954

Freddie Ayer and Anthony Grayling at a Duckworth Christmas party

Colin's office in Duckworth's premises at The Old Piano Factory, Camden Town

Colin with Beryl
Bainbridge at his house
in Gloucester Crescent

Colin in the sitting room at Gloucester Crescent

Colin and Beryl at the dining table at Gloucester Crescent

Colin with Brian
McGuinness

Colin reads from Gibbon's *Autobiography* to the assembled guests in his garden, at the party to celebrate the 200th anniversary of the completion of the *Decline and Fall of the Roman Empire*

Deborah Blake and Helen Muir at the Gibbon party

Colin ready for the first guest to arrive at a Duckworth Christmas Party

Colin and Andrew Barrow at a party at Gloucester Crescent

Arthur, Thomas, Stoddard Martin and William in the garden at Gloucester Crescent

The Boardroom Coup, 1992: Anna and Colin with their supporters

The Boardroom Coup: *(left to right)* Stephen Hill, Colin, Richard Mullen, Beryl, Melvyn Fairclough and John Haycraft

notice, cozy up to the 'heart of Europe'. And then what? Colin as publisher promoted a book by Bill Cash, the rogue Tory MP trying to block more Europeanisation after Mrs Thatcher's fall. He had also published an account of that fall in leftie Alan Watkins' *A Conservative Coup*. Yet, as if trying to hedge an uncongenial political bet, he turned Majorite to the extent of publishing what one reviewer called 'the Mein Kampf of the '90s': the Prime Minister's brother's memoirs.

An appearance of man flailing for ideological direction. An appearance of nation 'twisting slowly, slowly in the wind', to use President Nixon's Watergate phrase. Did Colin know what he wanted? Yes. He wanted to get away from his creditors and back to being a gentleman English publisher, or English gentleman publishing honest, intelligent books, without accountants breathing down his neck. But breathe they did. The wind of their breath became a monsoon. On the day the pound fell out of the European Exchange Rate Mechanism, Colin remarked that he would be the next after Chancellor Lamont to climb to the top of the Post Office Tower and throw himself off.

He lived on wit, adrenalin, too much coffee, strong drink, small cigars, flexed nerves and a ready laugh. There was no money. There hardly ever had been. With seven children (two dying) and employees and authors to look after, the jovial impecuniosity of an educated younger son was a perpetual Achilles heel. 'Maugham wrote for solicitors' wives,' he said to me of the most successful British author of the waning Empire. Such scorn was misplaced. At least, he might have heeded Maugham's memorable dictum that money is the sixth sense, without which the other five are not of much use. In a publisher and paterfamilias, it might have been a first law. But Colin sometimes reminded one of the ploughed-under Polish *Szlachta*, who turned Communist because of an ancient contempt for usury. 'We never concerned ourselves about money,' a member of this class once shocked me by saying. 'We let our Jews take care of that for us.'

Money is faeces, Freud is supposed to have said. Colin would have liked it to have been so. It was a flaw – perhaps the flaw. On the other hand, perhaps it was principally history that was against him, as of many of his type in his time. Fifty or seventy or a hundred years ago, England's commerce produced such a surplus of wealth that many gentlemen publishers could exist, if for little more than to amuse and edify a handful of chums. But culture is a luxury when rarefied; and a class in decline has a tortuous task sustaining its wilder flights. Perhaps this is the reason au fond that so many came for Colin's Requiem. In his demise, they saw the pagaent of decline of their own fondest, non-remunerative aspirations.

Still, it was not failure. He had fought on. He had produced titles: quirky yet solid, scholarly works that nobody else would have published. A history of the Vlachs. A psychological study of whipping in the Victorian era. The condition of women in Renaissance Portuguese colonies. Books for the curious; nooks and crannies of human behaviour – 'The Man Who Mistook His Wife for a Hat'. An account of the revival of the classics in nineteenth-century Germany. *The Sayings of Sydney Smith* and *The Sayings of Trollope* (Anthony, not Joanna). Ridiculous titles in comparison with the sex-and-shopping handbag-stuffers of airport news-stands; yet not unimportant. Colin would rewrite the inchoate and turn an author's speculations into a credible text: *The Ripper and the Royals*. All was perhaps, at some level, a precocious child's game. But was it a game not worth playing? Dickens would have admired his Micawber-like zeal. He would also have rued his Bleak House end, in the clutches of lawyers, tax-officials and money-boys.

We passed from the great stone barn to the low stone house, which Anna had made a home-away-from-home for many. We helped ourselves to a buffet along the long, blond-wooden table in a dining-room looking over green grazing fields towards the hedgerow hiding the church. People who had not spoken to one another from the heart ever were mild and conversant. John Haycraft reminisced about how Colin had loved music, playing Bach on the flute excellently. Hang on. Barking Colin? A silver flute?! Had the man had an aesthetic streak he had failed to show us? I thought back to moments, more frequent in recent years, when – despite his expressed loathing for anything Romantic – he would sit in his corner of the dining-room sofa asking me about nineteenth-century dandies, whom he despised perhaps less than he let on. One of his grandmothers, he amused us by relating, had been dandled by Liszt on Wagner's knee.

'Or was it by Wagner on Liszt's knee?'

At any rate, he guffawed; and a contagion of laughter spread out.

Such laughter! Thomas echoed it in another part of the Welsh house, standing by Mum at the Aga. And Thomas would go on, making wicked jokes like his Dad's, though more as a trickster than dandy. ('I had too many children to educate one properly.') No son would carry on with the classics. None was likely to follow in the family firm, literature having been so entirely their parents'. Perhaps by intention, they had not been encouraged to it. At any rate, now an era was passing.

The Welsh afternoon was passing as well. Beryl and I went back to the churchyard.

'Bye, bye, Col,' she murmured over the grave in the voice of a guardian elf.

'It's awfully beautiful here. Do you think he'll be happy in such a transcendental landscape?'

'It's not him, is it?'

No it wasn't. But what was? *Where* was? Better this than some Hawksmoor church in the City, boarded up through lack of worshippers and with headstones vandalised.

'I suppose it's good that he's here, in the embrace of the family. It's what he wanted, isn't it? for Anna to "get" him; to clutch him up as tight as she could, so that he'd never be alone. He would have objected to what he was subjected to, but he would have been appalled if she hadn't've done it. He would have been worried about her.'

Arm-in-arm, we walked back to the rent-a-car, wondering. How would Anna get clear of his debts? What would become of the firm so fully shaped in his image? Son Ollie would go back to post-rock ventures in L.A.; Sarah hoped to follow to make videos. Thomas, between things, would look after his daughter in Texas, while his wife and mother-in-law brought in the bacon. As William reflected, it was the era of the 'new man'.

'Your sons are doing all right now,' I had said to Colin the last time I sat with him.

'Only because they've been saved by women.'

'You mean like you with the Abbess?' I joked.

He chuckled, knowing what I meant: Anna had recently received a large advance for a book of opinion on the Catholic church. And though the fall of the British male was not as he cartooned it, and his sons were by no means failing in their own rights, there was truth enough in Colin's remark to make the exchange less than blithe.

Yet despite the clouds scattered over their prospects, they shone out in our minds as we drove back down the M1. Each had a beauty and charm all his own, like their father. Above all, they were fun – much more so than a solemn-souled chronicler who pays all his bills. 'No one who has ever had to do with that family has escaped untouched,' Beryl murmured; and she knew. There was a luminous halo around them, as around us in their presence. They seemed as large and indelible as the whole passing pageant of England in our times.

And so to rest, dear glad Colin, we thought to ourselves. (That stoicism again: we couldn't quite speak it!) You, the father of so many unforgettable moments: you will live on for us like a Greek for the lesser Romans. Painless and swift be your passage through decomposition. Your spirit has its own immortality here in your works, your descendants and our memories.

Appendix

Appendix

On Not Knowing Greek, or Latin Either

Presidential Address to the Classical Association
delivered in the University of Exeter
on 6 April 1994

Colin Haycraft

1

Someone like me who finds himself in this august position can hardly do better than ape, however impudently – an ape, as the Greeks would say, in purple robes, πίθηκος ἐν πορφύρᾳ – the late A.E. Housman who began his famous Leslie Stephen Lecture on 'The Name and Nature of Poetry' by acknowledging two immediate duties. First, then, I thank those who have appointed me, for this token of their good will; secondly, I condemn their judgment and deplore their choice.

It is gratifying to me, none the less, to find myself in this celebrated university in the ancient city of Exeter – a city of which my only previous experience was six weeks' confinement in nearby Topsham Barracks when I was inducted into the army for national service during the exceptionally bitter spring of 1947, when there was snow on the ground till the Ides of May. As a veteran, long since an *emeritus*, I am grateful to you for this much warmer welcome here today. Are the barracks still standing? Are soldiers still drilling? *Cedant arma togae.*

In five weeks' time, on the Ides of May, we should be witnessing in Rome the ancient festival of the Argei, when the Vestal Virgins threw effigies of old men into the Tiber off the *Pons Sublicius* with the cry: 'Sexagenarians off the bridge!' As a *depontanus senex* of five years' standing – a *lustrum* marked by the censors in London with a propitiatory bus-pass – I would be thankful once again that the ceremony had long since become symbolic. I stand before you older than Cicero when he wrote his dialogue *On Old Age*, not quite as old as his main interlocutor, the Elder Cato, but the same age as his friend Atticus to whom the dialogue was addressed.

As I struggle in imagination in the waters of the Tiber, I hear in my mind the words of Edward Gibbon – the bicentenary of whose early death we commemorated three months ago. Summing up his prospects at the end of the second best book in the English language, his *Memoirs*, he writes: 'I will not suppose any premature decay of mind or body; but I must reluctantly observe that two causes, the abbreviation of time and the failure of hope, will always tinge with a browner shade the evening of life.'

'Tinge with a browner shade?' Is this an echo from Gray's soppy 'Ode on the Spring', in which I read the lines:

> ... Cool Zephyrs through the clear blue sky
> Their gathered fragrance fling
> ... Where'er the oak's thick branches stretch
> A broader *browner shade* ...?

(Putrid stuff. If ever you are in doubt whether at heart you are a Romantic or a Classic, just ask yourself which you prefer, of two contemporaries, Gray or Goldsmith? Dr Johnson was in no doubt. Goldsmith was a universal writer who attempted nothing that he did not adorn – *nullum fere scribendi genus non tetigit, nullum quod tetigit non ornavit*. Gray's pseudo-classical odes, on the other hand, were 'forced plants, raised in a hot-bed; and they are poor plants; they are but cucumbers after all'.)[1]

'Tinge with a browner shade?' My learned friend and neighbour Dr Jonathan Miller – who, in addition to his cultural attainments, has had the advantage of a scientific education, – tells me that Gibbon must have been thinking of the 'Claude

---

[1] Johnson's general opinion of cucumbers is not in doubt, 'for it has been a common saying among physicians in England,' he told his biographer, 'that a cucumber should be well sliced, and dressed with pepper and vinegar, and then thrown out, as good for nothing'.

Glass' or 'black glass', a small tinted convex mirror whereby Romantic painters, poets and travellers sought to capture a two-dimensional view of a three-dimensional scene and to recreate the sombre picturesque effects of Claude Lorraine and other landscape artists of the previous century. Whate'er the truth – and the commentators, needless to say, are silent – Thomas Gray, according to his journal, did, I read, carry with him – and indeed was one of the first travellers to do so – a Claude Glass. As we grow older, we must be careful to use it as little as possible. Rose-tinted spectacles are better value.

I should say at once that one thing I neither deplore nor condemn is the ingenious practice adopted by the Classical Association of alternating in its choice of President between a distinguished scholar one year and some worthy the next who, having had the good fortune of a classical education in his youth, has long since foregone the *vita umbratilis* of the groves of academe. The scholar adds lustre to the Association, and delights you with a learned address. Next year some eminent banker, broker, judge, diplomatist or prelate reassures you, by his mere presence, of the worth of a classical education – living proof that even today, the study of Greek literature 'not only elevates above the vulgar herd but can lead to positions of considerable emolument'.

I quote Dean Gaisford's hoary apophthegm in its simplest form, as it is recorded in those entertaining reminiscences of nineteenth-century Oxford compiled by the 'radical parson' William Tuckwell. It was the concluding exhortation to his flock in a Christmas sermon from the cathedral pulpit. Another source, I am told – but I have no reference to verify – gilds the decanal lily by making him add a fitting eschatological flourish, 'positions of considerable emolument *not only in this world but in the next*'. Half history is anecdote. As any ancient historian among you will confirm, the more ostensibly apt an anecdote is, the more apocryphal it is likely to be. Tuckwell's more limited version seems apocryphal enough.

As a mere publisher, I can hardly hope to compete with my eminent professional predecessors in the senatorial virtues of *gravitas, auctoritas, existimatio* or *amplitudo*. Publishers are tradesmen. It was ever so. The commentators tell us that the brothers Sosii, who shine in the manner of publishers with a borrowed light, *notho lumine*, in the *Ars Poetica* and, above all, at the beginning of that charming poem which concludes the first book of the *Epistles* – Horace's best work, it always seems to me, though some prefer the *Odes* – were of comparatively low degree. They were freedmen, like the author's father. We are told that they were brothers; but I have always liked to think that there was really only one Sosius – like the late Geoffrey Faber ('Smith' in Latin) who, when his partner withdrew, thought it better business to put himself into the plural and become Faber & Faber, Smith & Smith.

Trade was regarded by the Romans, or at an rate by Cicero in the *Tusculans,* as a sordid occupation unless conducted on a large enough scale and pursued *sine vanitate.* A small independent publisher like me, though not acting entirely, I hope, *cum vanitate* – at any rate not a *vanity* publisher – would have been regarded by Cicero as too plebeian or banausic to be standing at this *rostrum.*

Hype springs eternal in every publisher's breast. As D.H. Lawrence wrote to Duckworth's reader in 1913: 'If *Hamlet* and *Oedipus* were published now they wouldn't sell more than 100 copies, unless they were pushed.' But the word could derive either from *hyper* or from *hypo* – 'too much' or 'too little'. Perhaps we latter-day Sosii would do more for the cause of learning and communication if we chose *hypo*thermia rather than *hyper*bole as our motive principle. We should cool it, rather than overshoot the mark. When we write our blurbs (to use that telling trans-Atlantic onomatopoeia) we ought perhaps to model ourselves on the first of Theophrastus' characters, the εἴρων, or Ironical Man – a kind of proto-Wykehamist above the battle who never says quite what he means – rather than on his opposite, the ἀλαζών, the Boastful Man, or hype-merchant, who says more than you ever want to hear.

At one point in the *Nicomachean Ethics*, you will remember, Aristotle cannot find a name for the golden mean between understatement and exaggeration, but elsewhere he simply settles for 'the truth'. This would never do in publishing, any more than it does for Cabinet Secretaries, Attorney Generals or Ministers for Open Government. The authors, the *genus irritabile vatum*, would be the first to complain. In this university a couple of years ago you held a fascinating colloquium on 'Lies and Fiction in the Ancient World', in which the boundaries were examined between truth and falsehood in literature. But to an author this is a far less sensitive area than truth and false-hood *about* literature – or indeed, to a novelist, or publisher of novels, than *lies about fiction*. Try writing a blurb for Jeffrey Archer.

2

If I am to judge the 'state of the classics' from my worm's-eye view as a publisher, I have to say that it looks extremely buoyant – with regard to publications. There seems to be a greater number of good books published – and bad ones too, I am afraid – than there was in my youth, particularly in history and archae-ology.

I should make it clear that my youth consisted of reading Mods and Greats at Oxford. I was lucky to be at the most beautiful college in Oxford, Queen's – the only college built entirely according to the designs of Sir Christopher Wren – where I had the benefit of the generous Oxford tutorial system and of three excellent tutors, James Bolton, Guy Chilver and Tony Woozley, the first two of whom have sadly long since joined (what used to be) the majority.

Greats in those days, just after the war, was still regarded at Oxford as the best School for an undergraduate to be in, at any rate in the humanities. Indeed it *was* the humanities, *literae humaniores*, 'humaner letters', the term invented in the Renais-sance to distinguish classics from divinity. Its prestige was partly due to its very incongruity, for by a happy historical accident it combined more than one subject – Greek and Latin languages and literature, ancient history, and philosophy, which meant modern philosophy as well as ancient. The philosophers, having roused themselves from their dogmatic slumbers, were busily doing themselves out of a job by solving, or dissolving, all metaphysical problems. Philosophy, the queen of the sciences, told other disciplines what they were about. There was a healthy rivalry in those days between Mods and Greats, between form and content;[2] but with a loosening of the syllabus and an increase in specialisation this battle is a thing of the past, as remote as the Battle of the Mods and Rockers.

Specialisation is perhaps no bad thing for scholarship, but whether it is good for education or 'general culture', is another question. There is certainly a conspicuous absence today, in the matter of learning, of what economists hopefully call the 'trickle-down effect' of wealth from the top. Where there was once among the educated public a relaxed if distant familiarity with the classics, now generally speaking – and before generalising we may wish to invoke Aristotle's Lesbian rule (*EN* 1137b30) – there is either an outright hostility to, or an excessive veneration for, the ancients, particularly the Greeks.

The hostility stems from a satisfaction (φθόνος) in a 'classless society' that the classics, once associated with the establishment, are no longer pre-eminent. The veneration derives ultimately from the Romantics who, having exhausted atheism and revolution, were looking for an alternative religion. The Greeks, with their democracy, childlike spontaneity, Attic light and naked statues, filled the bill. Fortunately, that dawn in which it was bliss to be alive was also a new dawn for Greek scholarship, largely pioneered by Germans,[3] which enabled the Greeks at last to be viewed directly rather than through a Roman perspective-glass; but the excessive awe survives today among the half-educated who like to talk of Plato and mouth Greek tragedy on television. *Omne ignotum pro magnifico.*

Three or four generations ago, in 1925, Virginia Woolf, daugh-

---

[2] Now that so few people bother with the languages, it is all content and no form. We have come a long way since a regius professor could say: 'I knew the *Agamemnon* by heart years and years before I thought of asking myself what it was about.'

[3] From 1825 when, as Housman put it, 'our own great age of scholarship was ended by the successive strokes of doom which confined Dobree and Elmsley to the grave and Blomfield to the bishopric of Chester' until towards the end of the nineteenth century the English were concerned mainly with classical education (which is not the same thing as classical scholarship). For a difference of approach in our own day between Teutonic and Anglo-Saxon scholars, we may cite contrasting opinions of the sixth mime of Herodas, belatedly yielded up a century ago by the sands of Egypt: 'An obscenely lewd conversation between two women friends' (Prof. Albin Lesky); 'Two women talk together with an agreeable cynicism' (Sir Maurice Bowra). It would be interesting to hear your view, ladies.

ter of the critic and historian Sir Leslie Stephen, the first editor of *The Dictionary of National Biography,* and half-sister of Gerald Duckworth, who in 1898 founded the publishing firm with which I have had the honour of being associated, wrote a famous essay in *The Common Reader* (a title derived from Johnson) entitled 'On Not Knowing Greek'. Her drift is not always easy to catch – *quo, musa, tendis?* She was not the man her father was. But her burden seems to be that the true nature of Greek literature is lost to us, partly because of the remoteness of the civilisation from which it comes, but largely because we do not know the language and the subtleties of the words originally used.

She was right, if what she meant was that we cannot know Greek in the same way as we may know a modern language. But we should remember at the same time that Greek has never been very widely known in the west even in its rudiments, let alone its subtleties. Augustine knew virtually none. To Petrarch it was 'little more than a vision, a dreamworld' (Pfeiffer). Even Erasmus did not begin it properly until he was about thirty. Locke thought it unnecessary for a gentleman. 'Greek, Sir,' said Johnson, 'is like lace; every man gets as much of it as he can.'

What we are facing in this generation is something quite new, which would have shocked Johnson and even surprised Virginia Woolf: the loss, not of Greek, but of Latin. In the Renaissance, when Latin was the learned language in which Greek scholarship, like everything else, was treated, the humanists had a word for people who had Latin but no Greek: 'semiliterate', '*semiliterati*'. We, on the other hand, have become, I won't say illiterate – but 'Engliterate'. Eng. lit. for many reasons – mostly economic: it is easier to teach – has long since ousted classics, just as social 'science' in its various forms has prevailed over philosophy. We should all take pleasure in our literature, and there are several good scholars who interpret and analyse it for us (with tools derived from classical scholarship) though we may ask of some, What do they know of Eng. lit. who only Eng. lit. know? But in Eng. lit. departments at most universities today interpretation and analysis have long since given way to 'theory'. This is 'difficult' and obscure because the critics are ignorant of philosophy (except French philosophy), and it serves the critic's ego by placing him above the author.

There is thus a fearful asymmetry in the world of books. The publishers are bored with books, and desperately hype the author. The critics demote the author and elevate the book by deconstructing it, thereby rendering it even more boring. Meanwhile the hungry sheep look up and – [aposiopesis].

We should never forget that the best reason for a classical education is not so much that it 'trains the mind', as used to be so vociferously claimed by its defenders, as that it enables us to read, for their own sake, the astonishing chance remains[4] of Greek and Latin poetry and prose. These cannot come across to us – certainly not the poetry – unless we have some knowledge of the languages. Translations are useful, and can even be good, as cribs. But who wants to be forever paddling in wellies, however green?

The classics, particularly Latin, open a window on the past, not only on the ancient, pre-Christian past, but on the whole subsequent history of Europe which has grown out of them: read Gibbon. Nobody but a Philistine[5] would say that the past is not worth knowing about, unless he were making a debating point or arguing a thesis – εἰ μὴ θέσιν διαφυλάττων, as Aristotle would say. Not to know Latin, lamented the central character in *A Portrait of the Artist as a Young Man*, is to be 'forever a shy guest at the feast of the world's culture'.[6] Even the pioneer of modernism, Ezra Pound from Idaho, spoke up for Latin in his *Guide to Kulchur*, opining that it was 'on the whole' more useful than Greek 'to a thinking man'. (How did *he* know?)

---

[4] John Addington Symonds (1893): '... beneath the ocean of time and oblivion remain for ever buried stores of poetry which might have been sufficient to form the glory of a literature less rich in masterpieces than the Greek.' Very few Greek authors survive entire apart from Plato.

[5] When Mathew Arnold introduced this metaphorical appellation from the German (*Philister*), he preferred it to the French *épicier* which 'casts a slur upon a respectable class, composed of living and susceptible members, while the original Philistines are dead and buried long ago'.

[6] Did Joyce adapt or pilfer this phrase, I wonder, from his mentor Arthur Symons, who said that in Baudelaire 'the spirit is *always an uneasy guest at the orgy of life*' (my italics). Such 'parallel passages' have an unfailing interest for anyone brought up on commentaries.

And Latin remains an excellent school subject, whether or not it be continued at university. Its very remoteness – as a dead, inflected language – instills in the pupil at an early age a proper respect for words and their meanings, an appreciation of the *copia rerum et verborum*, and inculcates the revolutionary notion that the world did not begin yesterday, or even in the nineteenth century. It also teaches the essential art of using reference books: of knowing how to look things up (ἱστορικὴ τέχνη).[7]

Unfortunately, the decline of Latin, so far from being compensated by new life for modern languages, has been accompanied by their decline also. Modern linguists at university are the first to complain of a retreat from grammar in the schools, particularly in state schools. Oxford's new professor of 'language and communication', whose chair is sponsored by the 'media' magnate Rupert Murdoch, assures us that it does not matter whether 'media' is a singular or a plural. Perhaps not. But how shameful not to know. 'Why do purists grumble so much?' she asks, concluding somewhat impurely and with affected colloquialism: 'Language is just changing *like it always did*.' But who but the dullest pedant or purist believes that language is immutable? If he does, he will be disabused by a glance through the myriad changes of meaning and usage recorded in that supreme desert-island book, Liddell & Scott. Grammatical and stylistic rules, as everyone knows, are descriptive, not prescriptive – or prescriptive only in the way that they describe what logic or custom or taste requires. On the other hand, it is the worst cant to suppose that a knowledge of grammar is somehow incompatible with, or inimical to, 'self-expression'. The same attitude has prevailed, I am told, in art schools. Is a painter any the better for not knowing the rules of drawing or perspective? Many people, alas, still think so. Self-expression seems to be just another Romantic conceit. As Swift or any other good writer will tell you, the secret of a natural flowing style (εἰρομένη λέξις) is 'proper words in proper places'. No amount of sensibility can compensate for lack of sense: *scribendi recte sapere est et principium et fons*.

It is sad that Latin has to be defended at such a mundane level. But these are desperate times: one-eyed Hannibal is at the

---

[7] I coin this phrase on the lines of Socrates' μαιευτικὴ τέχνη, the midwife's or dialectician's – or publisher's – art.

gates. Some years ago a former Prime Minister, in her milk-snatching days, rose to an eloquent peroration in the House of Commons. 'For we that remain,' she was heard to say, 'it is close to midnight.' 'Just so,' someone remarked; 'if this is the educational standard of the Secretary of State for Education, what hope is there for we all?'

To say *me* for *I*, or *who* for *whom*, etc., may be justified as idiomatic and colloquial; but to err the other way round, as is done so often today by the uneducated, is embarrassingly ignorant, pretentious and genteel. We are rapidly approaching the condition of the inhabitants of Soloi in Cilicia whose sloppy use of language gave the Greeks (and 'we') a new word: σολοικισμός, *solecism*.[8]

And pity 'we' poor publishers who have to clean up the mess and wipe our authors' noses for them, as Thrasymachus offered to do for Socrates in the *Republic*: εἰπέ μοι, ἔφη, ὦ Σώκρατες, τίτθη σοι ἔστιν; 'Tell me, Socrates, do you have a nurse?'

The pedants of course are never at rest. While Greek – that 'musical and prolific language that gives a soul to the objects of sense and a body to the abstractions of philosophy' (Gibbon) – is reduced to an arcane specialism almost on a level with Hebrew, an extraordinary snobbery has developed among people who like to quote Latin. Last year the *Spectator* ticked off *The Times* for recording the discovery of some of T.S. Eliot's 'juvenalia'. But *iuvenalis* and *iuvenilis* exist equally in classical Latin and are often confused in manuscripts, and 'juvenilia' in its modern sense never seems to be found among the ancients. Nemesis was at hand: οὐδ' ἀλαοσκοπιὴν εἶχε. She had no 'Dutch ear', no *auris Batava*, as the Dutchman put it in his book of *Adages*, quoting a Spaniard (Martial). Lo, the *Spectator* scribes were found to have printed the phrase *obita dicta*. Did they think it meant 'famous last words'? In the country of the blind, said the scholiast, the bleary-eyed man is king – ἐν τυφλῶν πόλει γλαμυρὸς βασιλεύει.

This question of correct Latin is a tricky one. Some famous Latin tags are not even Latin. Take '*memento mori*'. It makes no sense, or rather not the sense intended. '*Memento*', imperative,

---

[8] The ancient grammarians distinguished solecism, incorrectness in the construction of sentences, from mere barbarism, incorrectness in the use of words.

when followed by an infinitive, can only mean, as in English, 'Remember to ...', 'Don't forget to ...': *tu regere imperio populos, Romane, memento*. 'Remember death' would be *'memento mortis'*. *'Memento mori'*, 'Don't forget to die', only makes sense as advice to a centenarian.

Some people even lament the decline of classical quotation. But Lord Chesterfield, the great Machiavel of social life, advised against parade of wit in public: keep your sword in its scabbard – don't wave it about and frighten the company. Besides, even in its heyday most classical quotation was about as spontaneous as the wit of the Algonquin Round Table. 'Just a bunch of loudmouths showing off,' said Dorothy Parker, 'saving their gags for days, waiting for a chance to spring them.' For years it was hardly possible for an author to present another with a copy of his book without immediately getting one back inscribed with a hackneyed allusion to the exchange of arms between Glaucus and Diomede in the sixth *Iliad* – 'bronze for gold'. The giving and receiving of presents, said Swift, is a delicate matter.

During the triumphs of the Liberal Party, the Etonian W.E. Gladstone and his Wykehamist colleague Robert Lowe would bombard one another in the House with well-prepared quotations from Virgil, usually involving the Trojan Horse. Lowe was the man who, as Chancellor of the Exchequer, levied a tax on matches, proposing to inscribe each box *'Ex luce lucellum'* – 'From light a little profit.' It nearly brought the Government down (if not the House), and some said that Lowe had only introduced the tax for the sake of his motto. Near my office in London is a fine old Victorian coal-fired electricity station whose function is proclaimed in large letters on the wall: *'E pulvere lux et vis'* – 'From dust, light and power'. Which came first, I wonder, the building or the legend?

3

To set my prejudices in perspective for you, I should say something of my own early education. 'Of all the practical arts,' said Mark Pattison in his *Life of Milton* (1879), 'that of education seems the most cumbrous in its method, and to be productive of the smallest results with the most lavish expenditure of means

... Every one, as he grows up, becomes aware of time lost, and effort misapplied, in his own case.'

Chacun à son dégout. Pattison, if we are to judge from his posthumous *Memoirs* (partly inspired by Gibbon's), was something of a neurotic – a *Heauton Timorumenos.* In my case I have nothing to confess but privilege. I was destined for a boarding school, 'the convenient and customary mode of English education', as Gibbon described it, though he escaped it himself owing to illness; and since my father was a professional soldier, I was put down for a school with a strong military tradition, Wellington College in Berkshire. Sadly, my father was killed when I was two months old. My elder brother and I were therefore entered on the Foundation. We were technically 'Heroum Filii', the sons of heroes – what the school was for. A *herois filius,* one step down from *Divi Filius,* was educated virtually free.

We were fortunate to be at the school during the war when the teaching staff was buttressed by an extraordinary array of temporary schoolmasters. One of them took a Prize Fellowship at All Souls by examination from the school and ended his career as head of an Oxford college. The two chaplains, who were brothers, also later became heads of houses at Oxford or Cambridge and regius professors. (The one who prepared me for Confirmation, you will be glad to know, was appointed to the Order of Merit.) Above all I remember Alan Ker, who before the war had been a Mods Tutor at Brasenose with Maurice Platnauer and later became a Fellow of Trinity College, Cambridge and wrote a memoir of Housman. In my last two years he was Sixth Form master at the school. To be taught as a schoolboy by a man of this calibre was an amazing piece of good fortune. He did not succeed in making me a scholar, but he gave me an idea of the meaning of scholarship.

Like others of his generation, Alan Ker had been taught at Oxford by Gilbert Murray; and I remember examples passed on of Murray's legendary command of the Greek language, such as his rendering into an iambic trimeter of a popular Australian moral precept of the time, 'Pep without purpose is piffle': ἄνευ προνοίας ἄπορον ἡ προθυμία. What was gratifying was not only the copied alliteration, but the nice use of the neuter and the tripping resolution of the third foot.

I also remember the line considered the most beautiful in Greek tragedy, whether by Alan Ker or Gilbert Murray (or both) I forget: the messenger's gnomic utterance at *Oedipus Tyrannus* 961, σμικρὰ παλαιὰ σώματ' εὐνάζει ῥοπή, 'It takes but a small tip of the balance to put to sleep old bodies' – and only five words to express it in Greek.[9]

Another instructor who influenced me profoundly was the Rackets professional, Walter Hawes, who was then on the brink of retirement – almost a *rudiarius* (he had been professional champion forty years before). He usually played in his braces and would often play the ball behind his back to save turning for a backhand – positioning himself like the poet Cavafy, 'motionless at a slight angle to the universe'. You should step into a half-volley and hit the ball back where it came from: if it came to you off the side-wall it should be sent back on to the side-wall, not wrenched to the front. Like Alan Ker writing Greek or Latin – or English – Walter knew that nothing could be forced out of its true path: nothing could profitably be done *invita Minerva*.

Is Rackets still playing? It was gratifying to visit the school the other day and to find that indeed it is, and that the classics, now under the expert care of a Queen's man, Richard Coleman, flourish likewise.

That it was possible to get a classical education at Wellington at all was something of an accident. When the great Duke died in 1852 and his son was asked what sort of public tribute should be instituted in his memory, he suggested that a bronze statue of his father should be erected in 'every considerable town' in England. But this idea of multiple statues did not appeal to the Teutonic mind of the Prince Consort, who favoured instead the establishment of a school for the orphaned children of army officers. (Children, I say: note that there was no reference to their sex – what ignorant people now would call their 'gender' – but girls, alas, were eventually excluded from the Foundation because of expense.)

[9] The most melodious line in Latin was nominated by Johnson as Virgil's *formosam resonare doces Amaryllida silvas*, the 'very worst' by R.Y. Tyrrell (in 1898) as Statius' apostrophe to childlessness in one of his 'creeping Sapphics', *orbitas omni fugienda nisu*. It is against absurd abstractions such as this that a study of Latin is supposed to protect us.

At first it was thought that these orphaned children should be taught subjects which today would be termed, to use another cant word, 'relevant'. Indeed one of the reasons listed by Prince Albert's admirer Charles Kingsley for sending his son Maurice to Wellington was that he would not be 'stupefied with Latin and Greek'. Latin and Greek, however, were all that the first Master, Edward Benson, knew. Benson – a diminutive, irascible *plagosus Orbilius*[10] who ended up as Archbishop of Canterbury – turned Wellington into an ordinary school which taught Classics.

Benson's favourite pupil at Wellington was A.W. Verrall who in the last century developed a reputation in some quarters, notably Cambridge, as a brilliant emender and reinterpreter of Euripides, though his 'baleful influence' (Housman) extended to Horace – 'the insufferable Verrall', as Sir Hugh Lloyd-Jones has called him, 'whose excessive ingenuity made ancient literature into a modern detective story'. According to Lloyd-Jones's predecessor, E.R. Dodds, Verrall's theories are 'a classic instance of that insularity in time which, blinding men to the uniqueness both of their own and past ages, drives them to impose upon the past the fleeting image of their own preoccupations'.

Rem acu tetigit – he hit the spot. It is hardly possible for us to make sense of any past society, let alone of one so distant as that of Greece or Rome, if we do not try to explain it to ourselves in modern terms. Dodds's own great book *The Greeks and the Irrational* is full of modern parallels. But this is very different from projecting our own prejudices back on to the society we are trying to understand.

The Victorians were notorious propagandists – as philo-

----

[10] It is interesting to note that all the best public-school beaters, from the 'pocket Hercules', 5-foot Flogging Keate at Eton (1809-34), in whose small bulk 'was concentrated the pluck of ten battalions' (Kinglake) – μικρὸς ἔην δέμας ἀλλὰ μαχητής – to his epigone Anthony Chenevix-Trench, were 'vertically challenged' (ἐλλείποντες τι τοῦ μέσου τὸ μέγεθος). Hence the egalitarian cry, 'Please bend over.'

Benson was a mightier wielder of the cane than of the pen, but his sons made up for it by severe *scribendi cacoethes*. To the eldest, A.C., author of 'Land of Hope and Glory', we owe the most soporific book in the English language, *From a College Window*, the River Lethe in print, whose very title is an incitement to its defenestration.

sophical radicals, utilitarians, imperialists, aesthetes or whatever. But the propagandist tendency is still with us. Extreme
feminism seems at last to be running out of steam, or hot air.
Women had no worse a time in Greek literature than men:
everyone had a bad time except the gods, θεοὶ ῥεῖα ζώοντες.
'Afrocentrism' is the latest manifestation of retrospective political correctness, as the American scholar Mary Lefkowitz showed
the other day in her brilliant lecture on 'The Deconstruction of
Greece' delivered as part of the centenary celebrations at St
Hilda's (sadly the last surviving women's college in Oxford). The
fascination to us of the ancient world lies not so much in any of
its similarities to, as in its patent differences from, our own. Our
understanding of it is hampered if we try to read into it arguments for our own hobby-horses – *Ludere par impar, equitare in
harundine longa.*[11]

The classical tradition at Wellington was confirmed by Benson's successor, E.C. Wickham, editor of the Oxford text of
Horace that you all possess. Wickham also compiled what was
for years the standard commentary on Horace, which, says
Fraenkel, 'has its merits ... but always clings to the proprieties
established in the Victorian age'.

Wickham was a mild man who married Gladstone's daughter.

[11] Andrew Marvell must have been unaware of this line when he composed
his verses on the attempted assassination of Archbishop Sharp of St Andrews,
'Scaevola Scoto-Britannus', in 1668, or he would not have written the unmetrical
culpa par at dispar sequitur fortuna Jacobos – 'equal blame but unequal fortune
pursues the James's': a neat antithesis if only *par*, like many monosyllables in
Latin (*bis, ter, cor*, etc), were short by nature. Unfortunately *par, paris*, like *lar,
laris* and – how many people know it? – *sal, salis*, is long. Unfortunately too, it
is sad to record, Archbishop Sharp was successfully assassinated ten years later.
Such are the perils of Latin verse. By contrast I have found no false quantities
in masters such as Erasmus – no mean poet, who wrote 130 Latin poems in
twenty metres – or Johnson (whose Latin and Greek poems are soon to appear
in an impeccable edition from Prof. Barry Baldwin). Milton, on the other hand,
despite all the ink and pedantry he threw at Salmasius, is full of them.

That Erasmus knew the quantities of *sal, salis* is neatly shown in the second
of two epigrams he wrote to accompany the gift of a silver salt-cellar to the Abbey
of Ghislenghien near Ath in Hainault commonly known as 'Val des Vierges':
      Virginitas nitor argenti, sapientia sal est.
      Virgo dat argentum; tu pater, adde salem.
'The shining silver represents virginity, the salt wisdom. The Virgin gives the
silver; you, Father, must add the salt.'

Perhaps he was a hen-pecked husband, for H.W. Garrod wrote of him in the preface to the revised Oxford Horace: τὸν δὲ γαῖα κατέχει *virum mitis sapientiae, cauti iudicii, disciplinae late conspicientis* – which, being roughly translated, means: 'He lies six feet under, a man who wisely never threw a plate, always found it hard to make up his mind and went around everywhere with his nose in a book.'

4

I was lucky to spend my formative years before school on the Riviera, at the foot of the Ligurian Alps in Italy and France, at Alassio and Menton (or Mentone), where my mother settled for a time after my father's death. It is to this period of my childhood that I owe my love of the classics.

My earliest memories are of Mediterranean vegetation (some of it of course post-classical) – mimosa, figs, artichokes, olives, vines, cypress trees, lemon groves, fields of narcissus – and the noon-day heat when

> The lizard, with his shadow on the stone,
> Rests like a shadow, and the cicada sleeps.

I quote from the first edition of *Oenone* (1833), before the poet was told that grasshoppers tend to get livelier, not sleepier, the hotter it becomes, and changed the second line to

> Rests like a shadow, *and the winds are dead*.

The lizard comes from Theocritus:

> ἀνίκα δὴ καὶ σαῦρος ἐν αἱμασιαῖσι καθεύδει

'When even the lizard slumbers in the crannies of the wall.'

Nobody seems to have told Tennyson (or Theocritus, for that matter) that lizards do not retire for a rest during the heat, any more than do cicadas, but being cold-blooded creatures seek out the hottest places. The first editor of Theocritus to have pointed this out, as far as I know, is Sir Kenneth Dover in his 'unpretending school edition' (to borrow Housman's ameliorative phrase) of 1971. 'There seems to be no limit,' Dover remarks, throwing in a further absurdity from Aelian by way of example, 'to the extent to which zoological folklore can triumph over observation.' The formidable A.S.F. Gow, in his monumental edition of 1950, is silent on the habits of lizards. So is R.J. Cholmeley (1901).[12]

The Greek for artichoke is σκόλυμος. Hesiod, you will remember, has a good passage about the heat of summer – ἦμος δὲ σκολυμός τ' ἀνθεῖ and so on – 'when the artichoke flowers and the ἠχέτα τέττιξ (the noisy grasshopper again) pours down his song from the tree ...

> τῆμος πιόταταί τ' αἶγες καὶ οἶνος ἄριστος,
> μαχλόταται δὲ γυναῖκες, ἀφαυρότατοι δέ τοι ἄνδρες.

'Now is the time when goats are at their plumpest and wine is at its best,' – and this is where the Stoic injunction to live in harmony with Nature (ὁμολογουμένως τῇ φύσει ζῆν) is hard to obey – '... now is the time when women are at their most eager and men are at their feeblest.'

The Latin for artichoke is *cinara*. It was also the name of Horace's favourite girlfriend. It is not always easy to work out the identity of Horace's girlfriends, but, as Fraenkel points out, 'whenever Cinara appears in a Horatian poem there is always a strong nostalgic note'. This note was forcibly struck, in an imitation of *Odes* 4.1, *non sum qualis eram bonae sub regno Cinarae*, by a former member of my college, Ernest Dowson (who, I am sorry to see from the *Dictionary of National Biography*, 'left after five terms without completing the papers for Honour Moderations'):

---

[12] Before condemning the ancients entirely for their feeble powers of zoological observation, however, we should perhaps pause to salute the Elder Pliny. In spite of the numberless libels propagated by this polyhistor against the animal kingdom, it should be remarked that he was at least right about ostriches. He does not make the absurd mistake, almost universal today, of supposing that they hide their head in the sand to avoid observation. Poor silly ostriches! As Pliny well knew, they merely hide their 'neck in a bush' (*cum colla frutice occultaverint latere sese existimantium*). Goldsmith got it right in his elegant *History of the Earth and Animated Nature*: the ostrich, 'finding all escape hopeless, ... hides its head *wherever it can*'.

> ... I cried for madder music and for stronger wine,
> But when the feast is finished and the lamps expire,
> Then falls thy shadow, Cynara, the night is thine;
> And I am desolate and sick of an old passion,
> > Yea, hungry for the lips of my desire;
> I have been faithful to thee, Cynara, in my fashion.

This is a convenient view of fidelity, to be sure, whether in this world or the next; and I am glad to read in the *DNB* that, like his friend Aubrey Beardsley and other figures of the last *fin de siècle*, Dowson died in the arms of Mother Church and now, like Beardsley, lies peacefully in his grave, all passion spent, high up among the lemon groves above Mentone.

To me too artichokes and the rest of the Mediterranean flora retain their nostalgic pull. I have often thought that people are drawn to the ancient languages either by an interest in solving puzzles – regarding them as a kind of algebra, in which the complicated grammar takes the place of mathematical symbols – or by a desire to evoke through beautiful language an old Mediterranean world. Both pleasures can be indulged, but for me the second has always predominated.

I am grateful to my mother for this early Mediterranean experience. As I never knew my father, she was my only living parent. According to Virgil, Aeneas carried Anchises on his shoulders out through the flames of Troy so that he would have the benefit of his father's advice during his long voyage to Italy to found Rome. The modern *philosophe* J.P. Sartre boasted complacently that he did not 'carry Anchises on his back'.[13] Nor sadly did I, but at least, like the younger Aristippus, I was μητροδίδακτος, mother-taught.

I was lucky to be brought up with books, especially books of history, which my mother liked. Two I remember in particular were the *Grand Larousse du XXme Siècle*, a concise compendium in six volumes of everything a sensible person might ever wish to know about the past or indeed the present (1925), and the six-volume pre-war Everyman *Decline and Fall of the Roman*

---

[13] Cf. Guillaume Apollinaire: 'On ne peut pas porter *partout* avec soi le cadavre de son père.' Like some of the best people, he was illegitimate.

Empire,[14] edited by one Oliphant Smeaton. I still possess the
copy of the Everyman which contains my mother's marginal
comment on one of Smeaton's more ridiculous notes. This is at
the beginning of Chapter 3, where the Historian is discussing the
problem of how public liberty can be preserved under a monarchy: 'The influence of the clergy, in an age of superstition, might
be usefully employed to assert the rights of mankind; but so
intimate is the connection between the throne and the altar, that
the banner of the Church has very seldom been seen on the side
of the people.' At the end of this sentence is inserted a little
superior number drawing the eye to the foot of the page, where
the reader expects notification of some parallel passage – from
Montesquieu perhaps or Voltaire – but is disgusted to find
instead the gratuitous pronouncement: 'Gibbon's remark here is
wholly incorrect – O.S.' Next to this in my copy are pencilled in,
in my mother's clear hand, with her conveniently parallel in-
itials, the countermanding words: 'Wholly correct – O.H.'

I have never discovered who this Oliphant Smeaton was (no
doubt a Ph.D. thesis is at this very moment winging its way to
my desk to tell me), but his notes are piously preserved in the
new Everyman edition of the first three volumes put out this
year in a feeble attempt to celebrate the bicentenary which is
saved only by its excellent new introduction by Gibbon *redivivus*,
Hugh Trevor-Roper.

Smeaton's notes provided me with an early warning of what
that great art-form, the commentary, is *not*. Needless to say,
when his author makes a mistake of fact Smeaton is silent – an
ox, as it were, on his pen. Summing up the career of Gregory the
Great, Gibbon admiringly says that Gregory was the last pope to
be canonised. Here was a chance for Smeaton to shine. Even
without benefit of J.N.D. Kelly's masterly *Dictionary of the
Popes*, he could have told us that at least a dozen pontiffs were
canonised between the death of Gregory and the birth of Gibbon.
But Smeaton is silent. (To be fair, so are all the other editors
whom I have consulted – including Bury.)

[14] I am flattered to find myself in the company of the great U. von
Wilamowitz-Moellendorff, who wrote to Murray in 1908: 'It is now forty years
since I first acquired for my library as my first book of learning in the English
language, Edward Gibbon's immortal history.'

I am glad to have the opportunity to recall my mother. Very few ancients mention theirs. There are plenty who mention other people's mothers in order to jest at their origins. The comic poets delight in telling us that Euripides' mother was a herb-seller. Aeschines and Demosthenes indulge in orgies of reciprocal maternal abuse in the ripe tradition of the Athenian law courts. In all Cicero's voluminous works there is no mention of his mother Helvia, though according to Plutarch she was a perfectly acceptable Roman matron. Similarly, the autobiographical Horace, while extolling his father in a famous eulogy, says not a word about his mother; we don't even know her name.

It is not till the decay of taste that mothers come into their own. Marcus Aurelius (who 'gave lessons in philosophy in a more public manner than was perhaps consistent with the modesty of a sage or the dignity of an emperor') smugly thanks his mother at the beginning of the *Meditations* for making him so pious, abstinent and frugal. Ausonius writes a touching 8-line verse to his mother in the *Parentalia*: she was 'serious-minded yet friendly, sober yet jolly' – and she was *lanifica*: she was good at knitting, or at any rate at spinning. By the time we reach Augustine and his sainted Monica, we are heartily sick of the whole subject of maternal influence. These mother's-boys should all have been packed off to boarding school.

5

Many of you no doubt have been racking your brains to think of the Greek for 'political correctness'. As far as I can work out, it was not a very Greek idea – though we must remember the character in Plato who went by the pompous name Euthyphro, 'Straight Thinker', and got his comeuppance from Socrates. It seems to have established itself with the disastrous growth of monotheism, when correct opinions (ὀρθαὶ δόξαι) became important in theological debate and the Orthodox party of Athanasius prevailed over the Arians at the Council of Nicaea in 325. The Arians became heretics – a dirty word[15] for people who were

[15] 'Eretici!' was the abusive cry of disappointed beggars as they ran after the carriages of tight-fisted tourists in nineteenth-century Italy (according to Samuel Butler).

politically incorrect because they wished to exercise choice, or αἵρεσις, which to the ancient Greeks was the hallmark of intellectual freedom. Is political correctness then just another case of 'the triumph of barbarism and religion'? As it is American in origin, perhaps we should say 'the triumph of barbarism and *fundamentalist* religion'.

'Back to Basics' seems easier to reconcile with antiquity. For a historical parallel we could look to the Roman sumptuary laws. These dated from attempts to control the importation of Greek luxury after the Carthaginian wars, and culminated in the puritanical zeal of the Emperor Augustus which produced, at one end, the incomparable *Georgics* of Virgil, with their message of 'back to the land' and, at the other, the sad banishment of Ovid – the last great European poet before Chaucer – to the back of beyond, in Eastern Europe, for his *'carmen et error'*.

We do not know exactly what the error was, though it was connected somehow with the adultery of the Emperor's granddaughter; but at least we still possess the *carmen*, the great three-decker didactic poem the *Ars Amatoria*,[16] that universal manual of seduction for both sexes – the first two books for (the) *hoi polloi* and the last for (the) *hai pollai* – which remains a useful guide today for anyone wishing to write tolerable Latin elegiacs.

May I quote an astute remark of the late Camden professor Sir Ronald Syme who, in the interests of precision, rebuked a fellow scholar for a ponderous statement that 'love elegy more or less died with Ovid'. 'The term "more or less",' remarks Syme, 'often a harmless enclitic, or mere evasion, ought not to be attached to asseverations deemed important.' Quite so. Syme, the most learned and readable Roman historian since Gibbon, was a New Zealander. He thus fulfilled Gibbon's 'pleasing hope' that there would arise 'in some future age, the Hume of the Southern Hemisphere'.

---

[16] Wittily translated for Penguin by Peter Green.

6

Let me end with a few examples of the *lapidary* quality of these two dead languages – their suitability for inscription on stone.

Take epitaphs. In my Oxford college, affixed to the wall of the Hawksmoor library, is a memorial to those killed in the Great War with the two immortal words INVICTIS PAX, 'Peace for the unconquered'.

Opposite is a memorial to those who died in the Second War, many of whom we are commemorating this year in the fiftieth anniversary of D-Day: four lines in the vein of Simonides written by the great scholar Edgar Lobel, a life-long Fellow of the college:

ΤΟΥΤΩΝ ΤΟΙΟΥΤΩΝ ΤΕ ΚΑΤ᾽ ΑΙΘΕΡΑ ΚΑΙ ΚΑΤΑ ΠΟΝΤΟΝ
ΚΑΙ ΚΑΤΑ ΓΗΝ ΑΡΕΤΗ ΣΩΣΕ ΦΑΝΕΙΣΑ ΠΑΤΡΑΝ
ΠΑΡ Δ᾽ ΗΒΗΝ ΕΒΑΛΟΝΤΟ ΚΑΙ ΕΣ ΤΕΛΟΣ ΩΠΑΣΕ ΔΑΙΜΩΝ
ΤΟΙΣ ΜΕΝ ΝΟΣΤΟΝ ΕΧΕΙΝ ΤΟΙΣΙ ΔΕ ΤΗΝΔΕ ΛΙΘΟΝ.

'The shining courage of these men and others like them saved their country on land and sea and in the air. They put their young lives at risk, and in the end the deity granted – to some return, and to others this stone.'

From the epitaph to the sundial. From the sublime to the ridiculous, you may say: from ὕψος το βάθος. There is indeed something faintly ridiculous about sundials. As Pliny pointed out, they could hardly be relied upon to tell the time even when the weather was clear. They were superseded, he adds, by water clocks – themselves somewhat unreliable and inconsistent with one another, if we are to believe the author of *The Pumpkinification of Claudius*, who says it was easier to get agreement between philosophers.[17]

The art of writing sundial mottoes received a fatal blow from

---

[17] But what of our own latest technological absurdity, the wind turbine? Many of these hideous instruments adorn your countryside here in Devon as elsewhere, and are of no more use on a calm day than a sundial in a thunderstorm. As the paroemiographer put it, you might as well try to catch the wind in a net – ἄνεμον δικτύῳ θηρᾷς.

a Duckworth author, Hilaire Belloc, who suggested a number of suitable couplets, notably

> I am a sundial, and I make a botch
> Of what is done far better by a watch.

There is no record of sundial mottoes among the ancients; but since the Renaissance, if not before, classical authors have been ransacked for lapidary phrases to point a moral on the *topos* of time's waste.

On his dial in the front quad of All Souls, Sir Christopher Wren inscribed the words *'pereunt et imputantur'*, 'the days pass and are put to your account'. The same legend is to be seen on a curious clock in your cathedral here in Exeter. I wonder how many visitors to Exeter Cathedral – or, dare I add, how many Fellows of All Souls – know that it is a statement, not of the Protestant Ethic, but rather of its pagan opposite: that it is a quotation from a beautiful 14-line poem by Martial deploring time spent in business which could have been so much better spent in travel or gossip or visits to (second-hand) bookshops ... *gestatio, fabulae, libelli* ...[18] To the Romans, after all, the word for business was ne*gotium*, a denial of leisure, *otium*.

My favourite sundial motto is the anonymous *'horas non numero nisi serenas'*, 'I count only the sunny hours', a beautiful hendecasyllable worthy of Catullus or Martial. Equally cheerful is the last line of a poem in the second book of the *Amores*, in which Ovid has described an act of dalliance at siesta time in a half-shuttered room: *'proveniant medii sic mihi saepe dies'*, 'May I often have such noondays.'

On this sunny note I conclude – with the words with which Sir Leslie Stephen concluded his Clark Lectures on 'English Literature and Society in the 18th Century', published posthumously by Duckworth in 1904: 'I hope I have not said anything original.'

Goodnight.

---

[18] *Gestatio* was travelling around in a litter. The nearest modern equivalent I can find is Johnson's 'If I had no duties, and no reference to futurity, I would spend my life in driving briskly in a post-chaise with a pretty woman...'

Contributors

Francis King is the author of more than two dozen novels and other works of fiction and non-fiction. A former chairman of the Society of Authors and international president of PEN, his autobiography was published in 1993.

John Haycraft is the founder and former director general of International House. He is the author of several books, including *In Search of the French Revolution*, and is now at work on his autobiography.

Elizabeth Rosenberg is a former book editor.

Richard Brain is a former book editor and has for many years been an editor at the *Times Literary Supplement*.

Neville Braybrooke is a distinguished poet, novelist, editor and journalist. His edition of *The Letters of J.R. Ackerley* was published by Duckworth.

Brian McGuinness is Emeritus Fellow of The Queen's College. Oxford, and former head of the Department of Philosophy at the University of Siena. His *Wittgenstein: A Life* was published by Duckworth.

Lord Weidenfeld became chairman of Weidenfeld & Nicolson in 1948. His varied and brilliant career is recorded in his autobiography, published in 1994.

Lord Horder is an author and musician. He was chairman of Duckworth from 1948 to 1970.

Beryl Bainbridge is an award-winning novelist, playwright, journalist and former actress. Several of her eleven novels, all published by Duckworth, have been made into films.

Oliver Sacks is an eminent physician and medical researcher, and the author of several books on psychology, including *Awakenings, A Leg to Stand On* and *The Man Who Mistook His Wife For a Hat*, all published by Duckworth.

Sir Hugh Lloyd-Jones was Regius Professor of Greek in the University of Oxford from 1960 to 1989. His books include *Blood for the Ghosts: Classical Influences in the Nineteenth and Twentieth Centuries* and *Classical Survivals*, both published by Duckworth.

Alasdair MacIntyre is Professor of Philosophy at Duke University, North Carolina, and the author of may works on philosophy, ethics and metaphysics, including *Marxism and Christianity, Against the Self-Images of the Age, After Virtue, Whose Justice? Which Rationality?* and *Three Rival Versions of Moral Inquiry*, all published by Duckworth.

A.L. Rowse is Emeritus Fellow of All Souls, Oxford. Poet, essayist, historian and aesthete, he is best known for his works on Shakespeare and the Elizabethans. His *Sayings of Shakespeare, All Souls in My Time, Four Caroline Portraits, The Regicides* and *Historians I Have Known* are all published by Duckworth.

Helen Muir is a novelist and writer of children's stories. Three of her novels, *Noughts and Crosses, Don't Call It Love* and *Many Men and Talking Wives*, were published by Duckworth.

Derwent May is a distinguished journalist and book reviewer and former editor of the *Listener*.

Richard Gregory was Professor of Psychology at the University of Bristol and has written and edited many works in his field. His *Illusion in Nature and Art, Concepts and Mechanisms of Perception* and *Hands-on Science* were all published by Duckworth.

Andrew Barrow is a novelist and journalist. His award-winning novel, *The Tap Dancer*, was published by Duckworth.

A.C. Grayling is Lecturer in Philosophy at Birkbeck College, London, and Senior Research Fellow at St Anne's College, Oxford. His *Berkeley: The Central Arguments, The Refutation of Scepticism* and *Introduction to Philosophical Logic* were all published by Duckworth.

Tom Haycraft is a journalist and travel-writer.

A.N. Wilson is a distinguished novelist, biographer, literary editor, book reviewer and writer on religion.

Melvyn Fairclough is a writer and researcher. His book on Jack the Ripper, *The Ripper and the Royals*, was published by Duckworth.

Stoddard Martin is the author of *Wagner and the Waste Land* and four other books about late Romanticism. He edited the Byron, Nietzsche and D.H. Lawrence volumes in the Duckworth 'Sayings of' series.

Zélide Cowan, whose drawings appear opposite the title page and on p. 126 of this book, is a writer and illustrator. She has illustrated four books for Duckworth, including three volumes of Alice Thomas Ellis's *Home Life*.